Listening to Your Baby

Listening to Your
Baby

A New Approach to
Parenting Your Newborn

JAY GORDON, M.D.

A Perigee Book

Every effort has been made to ensure that the information contained in this book is complete and accurate. However, neither the author nor the publisher is engaged in rendering professional advice or services to the individual reader. The ideas, proce- dures, and suggestions contained in this book are not intended as a substitute for con- sulting with your physician. All matters regarding health require medical supervision. Neither the author nor the publisher shall be liable or responsible for any loss or dam- age allegedly arising from any information or suggestion in this book.

A Perigee Book
Published by The Berkley Publishing Group
A division of Penguin Putnam Inc.
375 Hudson Street
New York, New York 10014

Copyright © 2002 by Dr. Jay Gordon
Text design by Tiffany Kukec
Cover design by Ben Gibson
Cover photo by Lori Farr

First edition: July 2002

Visit our website at www.penguinputnam.com

Library of Congress Cataloging-in-Publication Data

Gordon, Jay, 1948–
    Listening to your baby: a new approach to parenting your newborn / Jay Gordon.
        p.   cm.
    Includes index.
    ISBN 0-399-52785-0
    1. Infants—Care.   2. Infants—Health and hygiene.   3. Toddlers—Care.
4. Toddlers—Health and hygiene.   5. Parenting.   6. Parent and child.   7. Child
rearing.   I. Title.

RJ101 .G67 2002
649'.122—dc21

                                                                          2001054565

Printed in the United States of America

10   9   8   7   6   5   4   3   2   1

CONTENTS

ACKNOWLEDGMENTS

Nancy Ellis told me I could write this book. Then she showed me how. Then she made sure it got done right. Thank you.

I'm glad I am not limited to thanking one person but, if I were, it would always be my wife, Meyera Robbins. She always believes in me, puts up with me, and makes sure I don't stop growing as a person, husband, father, and doctor. I love you.

My daughter, Simone, is too wonderful for words and a better writer than I am. I love you even when (like a good teenager) you're not so sure if you like me.

I am very proud of my website (drjaygordon.com), and Cheryl Taylor White has done all the work and helped thousands of mothers and babies while I was busy with this book. Her husband, Brad, sons, Ryan and Joshua, and her daughters, Emerald and Brie, helped, too. Many thanks to Lisa Freeman, our superb, hardworking, time-donating webmaster, and to Leeya Thompson who shaped my final draft and moved the words that needed to be moved.

I have the best, most satisfying pediatric practice in the world thanks to my office staff: Ileana, Christy, Beverly, Lisa, Jennifer, Marci, Holly, Harriet, and Virginia. Thanks to Linda

Nussbaum, M.D., who takes great care of our patients, too.

The moms and dads and children in my medical practice have taught me more than I learned anywhere else.

Sheila Curry Oakes and Terri Hennessy and the other fine people at Penguin Putnam were tremendously patient and supportive.

Thank you all.

Jay Gordon, M.D., FAAP, IBCLC
March 2002

CHAPTER ONE

You're Having a Baby!

I chose to become a pediatrician because I realized when I was in medical school that what I really wanted to do was start at the beginning of life. I don't think I would have been happy as an internist who takes care of adult patients who have already developed bad habits during the first thirty to fifty years of their lives, and then come to me and want to be patched up or have me help them get better. I have found it more fun and satisfying to work with parents (even before they are pregnant) and their babies and get them all off to a great start.

I was trained very conventionally, but it was the experiences of my patients that taught me that the best way to raise children was not necessarily the easiest way or the way most pediatricians approach the early life of a child. My conventional training taught me that the child should be welcomed into the family and then eased off to the side, taken care of during the day but perhaps ignored at night, or fed on a schedule that is suitable for an adult but that isn't necessarily right for a child. I believe there is a different way to bring a baby into your life and your home. When parents come to me I offer as much advice as they need and offer them many options. I also help them to stay current on the latest scientific facts and research. Most important, I encourage them to follow their instincts. Remember, however, that much of what I will be saying in this book will apply to healthy, full-term babies because a baby who is unstable will need extra attention and some of the advice given here is not applicable. An unstable baby is one who is born either very prematurely or one who is sick. Often after a very hard or long labor, a baby might come out unstable, that is, unable to maintain its temperature well, breathe in a normal fashion or maintain good oxygenation, or maintain a good heart rate, or later on, one who can't eat well.

I believe in something called *attachment parenting*. Attachment parenting begins at birth when you respond as much as possible to your baby. You pick up your baby, you cuddle and feed your baby, and then you cuddle some more. Attachment parenting means you stay in very close contact with your baby, taking your baby with you almost everywhere you go. Attachment parenting is in contradistinction to scheduled parenting, the method of parenting where a baby gets picked up and fed every three hours or where the parents leave the house very early and the baby is left with a baby-sitter. Attachment parenting encourages parents to build and maintain a close relationship with their baby by being there for it at all times. "Attachment parents" create a baby-centered home where the baby is breast-fed and sleeps in the "family bed." Our American cultural context for child rearing, unlike other cultures, does not support attachment parenting which means you attach your child to your life and attach *your* life to your child's. It means to follow your instincts as you raise your child. Attachment parenting usually involves devoting a tremendous amount of time and energy to being a parent, realizing that it is the most important job you will ever do. It's not just a nine-to-five daytime job but one that involves a lot of nighttime work as well. An example of being an attached parent is to "wear" your child in a sling or pack so the child can go with you wherever you go, whether accompanying you in your chores around the house, to the store, or to a concert. After all, the baby accompanied you everywhere before birth. Now you can provide an intimate and safe outer womb for it to continue its growing awareness of the world.

Parenting is the hardest, most wonderful job you could ever ask for and it starts well before the baby comes home.

Parenting during Pregnancy

While it may sound strange to speak of "parenting" during pregnancy, I believe that parenting starts with respecting your baby's needs right from the beginning. By paying close attention to those needs, you will be giving your baby the comfort and love it needs to grow and develop.

Before you get pregnant, there are many things to think about—your own good health, your relationship with your partner, and the level of flexibility you will have during the baby's first year or two of life.

A woman who is thinking of having a baby needs to know that during the pre-pregnancy period, moms-to-be need to take B vitamins, including folic acid. Folic acid has been widely reported to help in the prevention of certain birth defects. Many women do not know that they should begin taking multivitamins *prior* to becoming pregnant, not when they find out they are pregnant, because they can decrease certain birth defects in the central nervous system anywhere from 20 to 50 percent with the right doses of vitamins. Excellent health will lead to a higher success rate in pregnancy. If you are planning to become pregnant or are already pregnant, you should consult with your doctor before taking any vitamins or other supplements.

I often meet moms after the baby is born or when the baby is two months old or six months old. They may not have followed what I think would have been an ideal course through pregnancy and during the first few months of parenting. I tell them to do the best they can. For example, if the mother has not breast-fed for awhile, relactation is possible even though some people regard this as unusual or difficult. I've had parents who put their baby on a schedule for a period of time, realized it didn't feel good and then, instead of scheduling the baby, they decided to pick up the baby and hug the baby more. I've even had parents come in who wanted to know more about the family bed, because although their babies slept in the crib initially, they realized the family bed was somewhat safer and felt better to them.

To start, either before you get pregnant or when you discover you are pregnant, it's important to know what kind of health you are in, and whether or not there is a family history of diseases or disorders. Is there a history of allergies, asthma, or cardiac disease—particularly early cardiac disease? It is important to work closely with your obstetrician or midwife to get the right care and nutrition during your pregnancy. Your nutrition will have a significant impact on your baby's health. It's never too early (or too late) to follow healthy nutrition practices. For example, there is evidence that if you eliminate dairy products and peanuts from the foods you eat during pregnancy, you avoid sensitizing your baby to those foods in utero. In studies, it was found that when these foods were eliminated during the third trimester, babies had lower rates of allergies and asthma. Further research shows that eliminating dairy products during the second trimester also leads to fewer babies who were allergic. I feel that if eliminating dairy products in the second and third trimesters leads to fewer allergies, then eliminating them in the first trimester would be beneficial as well. Remember, what you eat during pregnancy turns into your baby. One of the ultimate gifts you can give your child is good nutrition during pregnancy, as well as during the rest of the child's life.

I encourage mothers to eat whole foods during pregnancy (and beyond, as what is eaten turns into breast milk). There are books that prescribe "one hundred grams of protein" or other kinds of diets. These books were clearly written by male physicians who had never experienced morning sickness or thrown up for five or six weeks. It is very hard for a pregnant woman to eat one hundred grams of protein. A mother should consume a very healthy diet with a reasonable amount of protein, which includes fruits, vegetables, whole grains, beans, pasta, tofu, chicken (in moderation), and very little, if any, sugar.

I personally like a somewhat non-American diet that is low in meat and dairy products, because eating whole foods is better than eating refined foods. When you eat whole grains and fresh fruits and vegetables you tend to get a lot of vitamins and nutrients per calorie. When you eat refined foods or high-fat foods, you get a lot of calories per vitamin. I recommend getting as many nutrients as possible without getting a lot of fat.

It is impossible to talk about nutrition during pregnancy without talking about weight gain. There has always been controversy about how much weight a woman should gain during pregnancy. Most people agree that a mother should eat what makes her feel good and should gain a moderate amount of weight. Again, your doctor or midwife will monitor your weight gain and work with you to achieve the weight that is right for you and your baby.

During pregnancy the baby is exposed to the mother's bloodstream, so everything the mother eats, the baby gets. Likewise, whatever the mother drinks, the baby also gets. If the mother drinks a glass of wine, the baby is exposed to the glass of wine. After the baby is delivered, the mother's liver can detoxify a certain amount of alcohol and the breast tissue can also detoxify a certain amount of alcohol. If a tiny bit of alcohol gets into the baby's stomach and absorbed, the baby can handle it. There is great danger to a baby whose mother is a heavy drinker but no danger to a baby whose mother is a moderate or light drinker. It's accepted by almost every single major expert in the area of pediatrics on breast-feeding that a mother who drinks a reasonable amount of alcohol, that is a glass of wine or beer with dinner, does not expose her baby to any toxic amount of alcohol. This is a generally, almost universally accepted point of view. You should have the best possible nutrition and habits but if you drink a glass of wine or beer once in a while, or need to take Tylenol or antibiotics—these habits or medications do not really affect the baby. Of course, it is important to let any doctor who is prescribing medication know that you are pregnant or breast-feeding.

Unfortunately, there is published research that confuses people. The *New England Journal of Medicine* published a study some years ago linking regular drinkers with diminished or delayed motor skills in their one-year-old children. In my experience, someone who admits to being a regular drinker is not a person who drinks a glass of wine or two. This is a person who typically drinks fairly heavily. If you drink heavily or take any medications or drugs not approved by a physician, you need to think about changing your lifestyle. Likewise, if you eat very poorly, not only will you be less healthy but your baby will pick up your bad habits. It is not fair to do that to your child.

Important Relationships during Pregnancy

Your pregnancy should be as pleasant as possible. This might sound like a silly recommendation to some people, because a lot of women throw up during the first month or two, or even throughout, their pregnancies. Many women are more than a little bit stressed. I recommend forming relationships that will decrease the stress and increase the positive aspects of your pregnancy.

The first relationship you have is with your baby's father. During pregnancy this relationship can grow and become more harmonious and filled with love. This is your baby and you have both participated in its creation. Talk to each other. Communicate as much as possible. If there are issues to discuss—the baby's name or whether or not to circumcise—get them on the table and talk about them. Get as much advice as you can. The relationship between the parents should be open and there should be lots of communication.

The married couple who successfully becomes pregnant embarks on a very challenging journey. The old adage "Let's have a baby and see if we can keep the relationship together" is obviously out of date and was never much good anyway. There is no better test of a marriage's strength than having a baby. You lose sleep and most of your spare time. If a relationship is not good, it is not a good idea to have a baby. A baby will increase the stress in an already unstable situation. If a marriage is good and strong it will withstand the stresses of the first few months and first year after having a baby.

The second relationship during pregnancy is with your obstetrician or midwife. Your doctor is your coach but he or she is also your employee. There are some doctors who try to fool you into thinking that it is *their* pregnancy. It is not. It is *your* pregnancy. You should get your doctor's advice and information based on his experience, training, and knowledge. Don't let what the doctor says go against your instincts. If it doesn't feel right to you to be doing something, don't do it. You need to seek good advice. Some of the most confused moms and dads who I talk to are getting advice they don't like from their obstetricians or midwives. Again, it is your pregnancy and should proceed the way you want it to work. Your pregnancy should be filled with positive energy, and the planned delivery should be the kind of delivery that you want to have. When you choose your doctor or midwife and hospital, make sure they understand the way *you* want your pregnancy and the birth of your child to go.

There is a lot of new technology regarding pregnancies, everything from amniocentesis to chorionic villus sampling (CVS) to multiple ultrasounds. There are high-resolution ultrasounds that allow us to see things that we never saw before on an ultrasound. Incidentally, I have seen more people scared by ultrasound findings than helped by them. A lot of babies have little spots on their kidneys or hearts that don't look right to the ultrasonographer, although nothing is wrong. Because the technicians performing the ultrasounds do not always explain what might be causing the spots, parents believe they are seeing kidney or heart damage. It is virtually never kidney or heart damage.

Whenever an ultrasound or any other test is done during

your pregnancy, first you need to know if it is necessary and second, once the results are given, if there is ever confusion about the test results. You need to make sure the person doing the test and the doctor interpreting the test sit down with you and explain everything, including the statistics involved. Rather than being told that this spot can mean kidney damage, you need to be told that this spot means kidney damage one out of five hundred incidences—or whatever the established statistic might be.

In my twenty-two years of practice I have seen virtually no ultrasound findings that actually mean anything to the baby. This does not mean that you should ignore the findings if you have an ultrasound or that you should not have the tests done, but please have the statistics explained to you very well. And don't let doctors scare you.

I often recommend an amniocentesis for any mother-to-be who is in her thirties because of the increased incidence of chromosomal abnormalities after age thirty-one or thirty-two. I don't think every mother of this age has to have one, and I don't think every mother has to terminate a pregnancy if there are questionable findings, but I think it is a good idea to have the information ahead of time. Mothers over age thirty-five or forty (and I see lots of them) may be at a higher risk for having problems, but the research is debatable. Some people say that a healthy mother at age forty has no greater risk than a healthy mother at age thirty, but this is probably not completely true. I recommend gathering information during your pregnancy for reassurance and in case you need to act on anything.

The third, and perhaps the most important, relationship you are forming is with your new baby. Babies can feel what you are feeling. They are part of you. Babies can hear very early during pregnancy. Talk to your baby. Play music for your baby. Enjoy some peace and quiet when you can. A baby will not be ruined if you have stressful moments during your pregnancy. A baby is not damaged if occasionally there are a lot of loud noises, but try to run your pregnancy, for the most part, in the nicest possible way for both you and your baby. Think of it as a way to hug your baby before she is born.

 ## Choosing a Pediatrician

- When you are choosing a doctor for your baby, I recommend looking for a pediatrician during your pregnancy. Ask your friends; if possible look in your neighborhood to find a doctor who is nearby. Again, find a pediatrician who's being used by your friends and their families, somebody they like.

- Find a pediatrician who is available in the way that you need him or her to be available. If you need Saturday appointments, you need a pediatrician who is available on Saturdays. If the baby's father is working late, you might need appointments later in the day.

- Find a pediatrician who you believe will support you in the way that you want to raise your baby. You don't want to blindly trust a pediatrician's philosophy. You want to do your own reading and research and thinking and decide how you would like to raise your baby, how you would like to feed your baby. It is my very strong point of view that you need to find a pediatrician who is knowledgeable and who is very supportive of breast-feeding because this is the cornerstone of good nutrition and good nutrition is the cornerstone of pediatrics and good health. If a doctor is not well-versed in breast-feeding, I think you should find another doctor.

- Find a doctor whose office looks good to you. Again, if possible, find a doctor whose office is close to you, although this is not crucial.

- Well-child care is done at two- to three-month intervals. Sick-child care is often better done on the telephone. Find a doctor who's got a telephone attitude and telephone policies that suit you.

- Find a doctor whose call schedule suits you. Some doctors are on seven doctor rotations, which means that you won't get your doctor on the phone except every seventh night. Find a doctor who will agree to see your child exclusively or almost exclusively. There are some large pediatric practices where you rotate among the doctors and you see nurse practitioners. This works for some people because they think it's great to have two or three or five good doctors and a nurse practitioner with different skills. Other people would like consistency and only want to see one doctor.

- Figure out what is going to work best for you. Ask a lot of questions. Ask around. Interview the offices. Sit in the office for ten or twenty or thirty minutes to see how it runs. See whether or not you like the staff. See whether or not the staff is polite.

- See how it feels to make a phone call to the office. Are you put on hold for twenty minutes? Are you disconnected? Find out whether or not the doctor returns his or her own phone calls and whether or not the calls are heavily screened by nurses. In my office the nurses screen phone calls, but nobody is told they cannot reach me.

The first time I meet a family is usually between the sixth and eighth month of pregnancy. We talk about the mother's health and what she has done during pregnancy. If either of the parents, or grandparents, smoke, I try to change that. Having a baby is one of the best reasons in the world to quit smoking. A baby's skin is as soft as can be. The membranes of a baby's eyes, nose, and lungs are delicate and they are very, very affected and potentially very, very offended by the irritants and the carcinogens in cigarette smoke. Babies and other humans subjected to secondhand smoke are more prone to heart disease and cancer. This is accepted as scientific fact and not just scientific opinion. Babies subjected to secondhand smoke from smoking households are more likely to become asthmatic.

I also ask the moms about their flexibility during the coming year. I explain that their baby will not be flexible. Three in the morning and three in the afternoon are equally good times for a baby to talk to Mom or Dad, and to eat. I am always unhappy to hear about a rigid six-week maternity leave. I don't think it makes much sense to ask a mother to work hard for nine months, work really hard for six weeks, get the biggest, loveliest smile from her baby, and then go back to work. It is a national disgrace that we don't have more flexibility built into the first year or two. The United States is one of the few countries that doesn't have paid maternity or paternity leave for the first year to two of a baby's life. If I do have a mom who has to go back to work relatively early, I talk to her about adjusting her work schedule because the more flexibility she has, the easier the year will go. The value to the employer is that they will get a happier, healthier mom as their employee.

I talk to parents about nutrition. I explain that great eating habits are one of the ultimate gifts to give a child. During the first two or three years of a baby's life you can set up the house, kitchen, and refrigerator to reflect good eating habits.

It is important that I have this discussion with dads present because in my experience, while Mom might have excellent nutritional standards, Dad may wander off and try to feed his child McDonald's. This is not to say that a child can't stray from good eating every once in a while. I do not have any philosophical opposition to birthday cake, Christmas cookies, Hanukkah candy, Easter candy, Grandma's cookies, or Halloween. I tell parents they can say to their child that on special occasions they can have some sweets but at home they will be having fresh fruit for dessert. Besides, fresh raspberries, strawberries, or blueberries are incredibly sweet unless you've eaten Oreos an hour earlier. I don't tell parents they have to bring carrots in a bag to birthday parties for their kid to eat instead of cake (besides it would probably traumatize the child more than the sugar rush). The idea is to establish good habits at home so that it balances out holidays or other transgressions.

On that first prenatal visit we will talk about car seats. Shop around for a car seat that's going to fit well into your car and find a store that will help you fit the car seat into your car. Car seats should be facing the rear until the baby is at least twenty pounds, and it should be placed in the center of the back seat. There's information you can get on car seats from the American Academy of Pediatrics (www.aap.org). If it's not at your doctor's office, there should be a copy of it at the store where you buy the car seat.

Some people like the convertible car seats that have a base in the car and can be unsnapped and taken out and used as a carrier. The government has done a good job at recalling the car seats that don't work. I recommend against a secondhand car seat; you don't know if it was ever on the list of car seats that were recalled from the market by the government. Buy a new car seat.

Babies may not ride home from the hospital unless they are in a car seat. This is nonnegotiable and is required by law. A baby being held in the mother's or father's arms is in danger, even in a low-speed collision.

Parents often ask me what they should have in the house to prepare for their baby, because they have seen those big baskets of lotions, powders, and creams. You don't need lotions. Babies come complete and do not need any after-bath cream; they also don't need powders. It is nice to have a gentle diaper cream such as calendula. I tell parents to try and use products without a petroleum base because it is a skin irritant. Talcum powder is no longer used on babies because we now know that it can severely irritate babies' lungs. I like products like bentonite clay powder or no powder at all. A little cornstarch on the baby's bottom works fine. However, if parents are concerned about rashes, I tell them to purchase a little bottle of grapefruit-seed extract, which can be found at a health-food store. Get a small plastic spray bottle from the drug store and dilute about five drops of the grapefruit-seed extract to an ounce of water. Keep this bottle on the changing table and spray it on the baby's diaper area. The grapefruit-seed extract inhibits the growth of yeast, bacteria, and fungi.

You don't need a lot of clothes for the baby. You don't need "onesies." I tell the parents that what they need to prepare is a whole bunch of diapers and some T-shirts or sweatshirts. Cloth diapers are a little bit better than disposable diapers; however, this is debatable. Nevertheless, there are some good disposable diapers on the market. I think that most disposable diapers can be more irritating to babies' bottoms, and many disposables contain chemicals like dioxin, which has been shown to be bad for the skin. There are organically derived disposable diapers which are mostly biodegradable, and if you are going to use disposable diapers all or some of the time, get those instead of the, unfortunately, less expensive and more available store brands.

You do need to take into consideration different clothing needs for different times of the year or areas of the country. Babies during the first week or so of life should be dressed just the way we are dressed, with a light layer, such as a light blanket, over them. After the first week or two a baby is quite capable of maintaining temperature during reasonable times of the year. When the temperature is about thirty-five or forty-five degrees, babies don't need to be heavily dressed, but just the way we are comfortable. If it's very, very cold out, everybody should stay inside. If it is moderately cold out, dress the baby the same way that you are comfortable, but put a hat on your baby because babies radiate a lot of warmth from the top of their heads and a hat will help them keep warm. They do not need to be very bundled. A very bundled baby gets hot and sweaty and rashy. A baby who is overdressed and is too warm won't have a very good appetite, especially during that first week or two of life. Babies do not get cold that easily. I like T-shirts and sweatshirts because they are easy, they are inexpensive, and they allow you good access to the baby's diaper without a lot of unsnapping. I recommend that when you go to your pediatrician's office for a visit, you do not use the "onesies" that snap in the diaper area because it is hard enough to examine a baby and keep a baby happy without having to reach in and unsnap everything.

I tell parents to be as personally ready as possible—especially Mom. Limit your chores during the first months after the baby is home. I tell moms not to turn down help from someone who wants to give them a hand, cook a meal, bring over a casserole, go shopping, do the laundry, or do errands. Be open to your needs. Imagine what you would do for a friend who just had a baby and ask for the same for yourself. I like doulas, and I like baby nurses. I think there is a lot of romance about doing everything yourself that first night, that first week of life and taking the best care of yourself, taking care of the baby and figuring everything out. There are doulas that can help take care of the mother. Taking care of the baby is the job of the father and the mother.

It is especially important for a single mother to get a support network developed before the birth of her baby. Single moms should ask around and get as much part-time help as they can. Get your friends on board. Don't turn down help! A lot of people will say to you after your baby is born, "Is there anything I can do for you?" and the perfunctory answer will be "Oh no, I'm fine." Don't say "I'm fine." Say things like, "I could use a little help with shopping this week," or, "Remember that dish you made for the potluck (or around Thanksgiving)? I would love some of that for dinner this weekend." People will love to help you, especially if you are a single mom. You might need some help around the house with cooking and cleaning and shopping. Don't turn down the help. Get your network of friends active and interested. They're going to be interested. If you can imagine yourself in the same position, you'd be excited to help them.

What to Expect at the Hospital

During the prenatal visit, most people ask me about hospital procedures. I work with quite a few good hospitals—and even though the hospital nurseries are good, your baby does not need to spend very much time there. The way my practice works is that I begin with a postnatal visit. I will show up at the hospital the day the baby is born to carefully examine him with Mom and Dad, head to toe, to make sure that the parents are comfortable with the baby's anatomy. I will make sure that breast-feeding is going well and that all the appropriate paperwork gets done. From delivery on, a healthy, full-term baby can stay with Mom or Dad. There is no need for the "separation" routine. Although hospitals function best on routines, we can nicely and easily explain to the hospital staff that this is your baby and there is nothing routine about her. Of course, if your baby is born prematurely or with other problems you will be very happy that you chose a good hospital and doctor capable of handling the nonroutine situation.

If you want to find out about hospital procedures, ask. All hospitals have protocols—the way they deal with the baby after birth. Some immediately take the baby away from the mother and father. Some hospitals take the baby away for two hours, during which they give the baby a bath, insert a catheter into the baby's rectum and another down the baby's throat, draw blood to check blood sugar and blood counts, and so on. These routines may be important for a premee or an unstable or sick baby; however, these routines get in the way of the first couple of hours with parents who have a normal full-term baby.

When researching hospital procedures, find out whether or not the delivery room will be somewhat under your control: Can you have the lights turned down a little bit? Can you bring your own music? Do they routinely shave women? Do they use IVs or give you the option of whether you want an IV for a normal vaginal delivery? Find out the procedure for cesarean births. Is the baby separated right after a cesarean? Is the father allowed to stay in the room for a cesarean? (He should be.) Is everything going to be explained to you? Again, can the lights be turned out after delivery? Can you be allowed some time with the baby even if the baby is going to be separated from you? The best hospitals do not separate the baby, mother, and father after a cesarean or after a delivery of any kind unless the baby isn't stable or is severely premature or sick. But you can ask. Many hospitals will have a written protocol.

Most babies are born at or near full term at thirty-seven to forty weeks' gestation. They will weigh anywhere between six and nine pounds. These babies do not need to be separated from their parents. A baby does not need to be taken from you to be bathed (you can do it yourself), or weighed (there are scales with wheels that can be brought to you), or to have their temperature taken (it can be taken under the baby's arm while you hold him). Your baby does not need to leave you. What your baby needs is to be with you and get started with breast-feeding. The earlier that good breast-feeding is established, and the more time you and your baby spend together, the better it is for the baby's health.

There are some hospitals that have some incredibly unscientific policies regarding the separation of the mother and father from the baby, such as placing the baby in a warmer and bathing the baby immediately. Also, there are a few hospitals that separate the baby from his mother if she has a temperature elevation. Because the mother and the baby share the same bloodstream before it is born, if she develops a fever, the chances are it is caused by a virus and the baby's best defense against infection is from the antibodies in the mom's colostrum. Remaining together and beginning breast-feeding is best.

I recommend the very shortest hospitalization. You don't need to pay too much attention to recent reports about the dangers of jaundice in newborns. Some hospitals respond to a slight yellow tinge of the baby's skin with blood tests and often out-of-date practices. Red blood cells in adults break down at about a 120-day cycle and in babies they break down in about a ninety-day cycle. That means in a baby there is a whole new set of blood cells every ninety days. As red blood cells break down, there are by-products, one of which is bilirubin, which is yellow. So, a normal baby will have a little yellow tinge to her nose and cheeks and it is completely harmless. Normal babies get slightly jaundiced. Breast-fed babies get a little more jaundice perhaps because they're supposed to. It takes a very high level of jaundice in a healthy, full-term, breast-fed baby to cause any problems. It is a very rare occurrence. Jaundice has for some time been, and still is, overtreated. Discuss this at length with your doctor. Jaundice is a normal condition in a normal, full-term baby of two to four days of age. A baby who is slightly yellow tinged, with yellow eyeballs, yellow cheeks, and who is nursing very well and vigorously, does not need any treatment.

In the past, there were babies born who had severe blood grouping incompatibilities. They were called Rh babies. Rh incompatibility is now almost exclusively a disease of the past. It used to be that an Rh-negative mother, when exposed to an Rh-positive baby, because the father was Rh positive, would be sensitized. The first pregnancy might not be a problem, but if there had been a miscarriage or an abortion, or a full-term pregnancy, that mother was not set up with anti-Rh-positive antibodies and the baby's bloodstream could be attacked, resulting in a severe life-threatening jaundice. Now we can desensitize the mother if she's Rh negative with Rogam shots that combat those antibodies so that even after a miscarriage or second or third pregnancy, the mother and the baby do not have this problem.

Keep your baby with you in the hospital and nurse your baby often. Reject the nursery's offer of bottles of water or formula as it does not decrease the level of jaundice nor does it increase your baby's ability to breast-feed. Instead, it gets in the way of normal physiology.

Routine Hospital Procedures

Vitamin K Vitamin K is necessary for the creation of clotting factors. A baby who runs out of Vitamin K and then runs out of the clotting factors can have a severe hemorrhage. This is incredibly rare. In my twenty-two years of practice I have never seen it, but it does occur and for that reason I think it's judicious to give the baby an oral dose or two of Vitamin K within the first few hours and days after birth. Vitamin K by injection is not necessary in my opinion, and in the opinion of many, many experts. Vitamin K is controversial because ten or so years ago a group of British doctors, trying to see what might be the cause of childhood cancer, found out that giving an injection of Vitamin K was associated with a higher risk of leukemia and childhood cancers. Other groups of doctors—the majority of doctors—did studies showing that this wasn't true, which led to that first group of doctors showing that their data was good, and the controversy continued.

An injection of Vitamin K raises the Vitamin K level extremely high. Giving Vitamin K orally does not give the same level of Vitamin K. The controversy involves the absorption of Vitamin K orally, whether or not babies spit it out, and how many doses of Vitamin K are needed. It is my feeling that one or two doses of oral Vitamin K protect a baby from Vitamin K deficiency.

Eye drops Eye drops are given to babies in case of gonorrhea infection. Because almost everyone is sure whether or not they have gonorrhea, I don't believe that most babies need to have this, and research published in *Pediatric,* the AAP's journal, supports choosing not to do so.

Genetic screening All hospitals will do a genetic screening test before the baby leaves the hospital. It is usually called PKU, which stands for phenylketonuria. This test screens for three very rare but treatable causes of mental retardation. Phenylketonuria is the inability to metabolize a specific amino acid (phenylalanine), which then accumulates in part of the brain. If it is diagnosed early, the baby can be fed a diet low in the amino acid phenylalanine and no brain damage will occur. The second disease that is screened for is galactosemia, which is the inability to metabolize a specific carbohydrate, called galactose. Again, if the screening is done and the baby is diagnosed with this condition, the baby can be fed differently and no damage occurs. The third thing that we routinely screen for is hypothyroidism, which is rare and occurs in only one out of ten thousand babies. If diagnosed early, a baby can be given supplemental thyroid hormone and the damage from this condition is prevented.

As your pregnancy progresses into the seventh, eighth, and certainly the ninth month, be certain you are clear about what is going to happen at the hospital and make sure that the people in the hospital are clear about what you want to have happen. You may not want visitors. You may not want interns at your delivery. You may want to make sure your doctor is going to be there for your delivery. You can get close to 100 percent reassurance from your doctor that she is not going to be on vacation. You may want to let the hospital know that you do not want your baby separated from you. You may want special music. You may want the lights turned down low. The hospital needs to know this in advance so you won't have to argue about it when you are in labor.

I hope that every parent leaving my office knows that they need not separate from their baby in the hospital. The nursery may be fine, the nurses nice, and I'm sure you have chosen a hospital that will take good care of your baby. But, separating a healthy, full-term baby from Mom and Dad increases the baby's risk. The more people who handle the baby, the more germs he is exposed to. The longer the parents are separated from their baby, the more likely someone is going to do unnecessary tests.

Should your baby be born by cesarean birth, do the best you can. Get as much help as you can from the nursing staff at the hospital. Make sure someone is sleeping in the room with you—most likely your husband—so that the baby can stay with you twenty-four hours a day and be brought back and forth to you. The nurses will help you with feeding and with diaper changes, and will help you with your recovery. Remember that bonding is not crucial in the first few hours after birth and you should not feel guilty if you are unable to do this. Moms who are separated from their babies end up having a wonderful bond and a wonderful relationship with their children.

Remember, you are going to be working hard, but the rewards will be commensurate with the amount of time and energy you devote to your baby's well-being. A positive future for your child is a tangible return on that investment.

CHAPTER TWO

Preparing for Labor and Delivery

I have attended a fair number of births—vaginal and cesarean—and the births that have been the most satisfying to the moms and dads have been the ones where the parents were in charge of the environment in the delivery room, which includes lighting and music, and where a relationship of cooperation and partnership has been established with the obstetrician. This partnership agrees that if there are any problems, the mother is going to listen to her obstetrician and will not question his judgment. But, if there are no problems, the mother needs to tell the obstetrician to listen very closely to what *she* wants. She may tell him that she does not want an IV if she is not sick. She may not want constant fetal monitoring. She may not want to be checked every few minutes to see where the baby is.

In order to get what you want I recommend putting everything in writing. Type out a nice list of everything you want and have a pleasant discussion with the labor and delivery staff as well as with your obstetrician. Make a list of how you would like things to go during labor and prior to delivery. Perhaps you would like them to know that you do not want to be shaved. Ask your doctor about this; it is rarely necessary. Perhaps you would like them to know you don't want an IV unless absolutely necessary. You may want minimal monitoring. Maybe during your labor you do not want people going in and out of the room or want people talking loudly. You may not want incoming telephone calls in your labor room. You may want the nurse to be someone you've met beforehand. You may want to get to know a couple of the labor and delivery nurses before you go to the hospital for your delivery. You may want to remind your doctor that you do not want to be separated from your baby after birth—as long as the baby looks good and is healthy, full-term, and stable.

Labor, to put it mildly, can be a somewhat incapacitating state of being. The father needs to be the mother's advocate and may need to intervene with some things in the hospital. He may need to interpret some of the hospital's requests to her. The father has a very, very important and powerful role here. He may also have to accept whatever moods the mother may experience during labor and the best way to do that might be by just holding her hand and being quiet (very quiet) whenever necessary.

Premature Birth

Some babies are born prematurely. Most people do not have an "average" pregnancy and their babies are born anywhere from thirty-nine to forty-one weeks—which is very normal. Forty weeks is given as the average gestation period. After thirty-six or thirty-seven weeks a baby may be considered full-term even though it is slightly early and slightly premature. After forty weeks, and certainly after forty-one weeks, a baby is considered post-date, or post-mature, and these babies have another set of risk factors since the placenta may not be delivering a blood flow as high as it should. These babies are at slightly higher risk. There are groups of doctors who now recommend delivering a baby or encouraging a baby with indication after forty-one weeks. This is not a universally held opinion, but we are moving very strongly in that direction. Forty weeks is the average gestation. After thirty-seven weeks the baby can be considered a full-term baby.

Some babies are born severely premature at twenty-five or twenty-six weeks' gestation and weighing one pound or less. These babies do not have high survival rates or good prognoses for future development. Newborn intensive care units can help these babies to live but there is some controversy about the levels of intervention required.

Many premature babies are born at thirty-two weeks' gestation. These babies almost uniformly do well. These babies are born with few problems but may need some extra assistance. They may need extra support in maintaining their body temperature. They may require special feeding because their intestinal tracts are not well-developed, or they may need oxygen because their lungs are not well-developed. If a delivery can be predicted at thirty-two weeks or so, some obstetricians will give the mother shots of steroids to rapidly mature the baby's lungs, which may save the baby's life.

Babies that are a little premature at thirty-five to thirty-six weeks' gestation also need extra care. They may weigh only five or six pounds. Their respiratory and digestive systems may be immature, they may not be good at maintaining body temperature, and they cannot suck or swallow as well as a full-term baby. If you have a baby at thirty-four or thirty-five weeks' gestation, you may not be able to keep the baby in the room with you all the time. However, a baby born at this time could be big and stable and be treated as a full-term baby.

Some babies born prematurely may also be born with unstable blood sugar and will need to be fed early. Not all, but some, can be breast-fed as if they were full term. How-

ever, some babies born four to six weeks early may need supplemental intravenous fluids to keep their blood sugar up.

If you have a premature baby it may not hit all early developmental milestones at the same time a full-term baby will.
In fact, much of what I discuss in this book will apply to full-
term babies, and a premature baby will not be on the same
"schedule." However, remember that all babies develop in
their own time and it will all level out between six and twelve
months of age. With a premature baby you will need some
extra help with breast-feeding, and you may need to use an
extra blanket to maintain his body temperature. Almost all
babies can stay with their mothers or have a short stabiliza-
tion period in the nursery and then room-in completely with
their mothers. Most of them can go home from the hospital
within a few days. Some of these babies need to stay in the
hospital longer to establish good feeding and to be sure the
baby is breathing easily.

Inducing Labor

I am raising this issue because, for a variety of reasons, some
mothers are induced to deliver early. This is done with a
chemical that ripens the cervix to make it ready for labor.
The mother is then admitted to the hospital and given intravenous Pitocin to induce labor contractions. Sometimes this

is done because the placenta looks like it is not doing well or the mother has run out of amniotic fluid or because the baby is getting too big. Quite frankly, sometimes it is done just for the obstetrician's convenience or because the mother thinks the best thing to do is deliver the baby a little early.

For whatever reason, these babies are sometimes delivered much too early. I do not recommend induced deliveries unless there is a strong medical reason for it, as I have seen babies who have been born when neither the mother nor the baby was ready. These babies often need extra care because they were not born at the time they were "supposed" to be born.

When mothers pass forty weeks' gestation, doctors begin to quote "studies" showing that there can be an increased complication rate and even an increased mortality rate if the baby is born one or two weeks late. This data is not complete and is controversial but most obstetricians hold to it nevertheless. Discuss this at length with your doctor. In fact, check in with your mother because there may be a family pattern of delivering babies at forty-one or forty-two weeks or there may be a pattern of delivering every baby at thirty-eight or thirty-nine weeks for as far back as you can research. If your family has a strong hereditary tendency to deliver a couple of weeks early or a couple of weeks late, you do not need to induce labor and you do not need to panic. You need to have a good relationship with your OB. If there is any doubt, your baby can be checked out by an ultrasound or by a "stress test" and can be followed more closely.

Cesarean Delivery

A baby can be delivered by cesarean for a variety of reasons. The most common is "failure to progress." This actually means "failure to be born." The doctor may tell you that he or she thinks your pelvis is not big enough, your contractions are not strong enough, or the baby's heartbeat is not regular enough. There are good reasons for doing an operation to deliver your baby. There are some people who think that the majority of cesareans are unnecessary. Be sure you trust your OB so that if he or she says it's time to do a cesarean you will be able to trust that the decision is right for your situation.

When a baby is delivered by cesarean, the mother receives anesthesia, which can be an epidural, a spinal, or even general anesthetic. The mother is therefore not completely able to interact with, hold, or get up and walk around with her baby right after he is born or for some hours after the birth. Many hospitals automatically separate the cesarean-delivered baby from the mother and the father and take him to the nursery for a few hours. Many other hospitals do not do this. However, even if you have a cesarean, your baby can stay with you, go with you to the recovery area, and can breast-feed within minutes or hours of being born. After a cesarean delivery, Mom will need to recover in the hospital anywhere from two to five days. During that time the baby can still be in her room—although the mother may need some extra help as she is recovering from abdominal surgery.

Virtually all medications that are given after delivery, cesarean or otherwise, such as pain medications and antibiotics, do not get into the breast milk in any quantity that will affect the baby. If your doctor advises you to take pain medication or antibiotics do so without worrying about your baby. There may be a minor effect on the baby, but there will be no harm to your breast milk or your baby from routine postoperative/postdelivery medications. Let your doctor know you are a breast-feeding mother and ask if the medication is safe for breast-feeding. Don't ask, "While I'm taking this medication, is it okay for me to breast-feed?" You *are* a breast-feeding family. There are medications that are not generally known to be safe for breast-feeding that really are. It is not as safe to artificially feed a baby, therefore the first priority should be, "I am a breast-feeding mother." The next priority is "what medication do I need?" Obviously in a life-threatening situation, priorities have to shift. Very few doctors are well-versed in medication in breast-feeding situations. As a result they tell mothers that they can't breast-feed while taking a medicine. They are usually wrong.

Babies are often quite alert at the time of birth. Shortly after and during the first twenty-four hours they take long naps of anywhere from six to eight hours. I strongly recommend and even insist that the moms in my practice use the baby naptime to nap themselves. I tell them not to entertain visitors. It is important to match your baby's rhythms all through the first day and into the early days and weeks of your baby's life. It is much easier for you to adjust to the baby's rhythm than to try and get her to adjust to yours. This is part of creating the baby-centered home and life. Part of welcoming your baby into your home is understanding the unique aspects of newborn behavior.

One of the concerns new parents have right away is that the baby doesn't appear to hear very well. This is normal. Amniotic fluid may have gotten behind the baby's eardrum and the eardrum may not vibrate very well. They are also often concerned about the baby's breathing. Babies make gurgling, snuffling, gulping, and wheezing sounds and in general, are noisy breathers—all of which are normal. A baby's airway is very narrow and even a small amount of mucus can cause a baby to whistle and wheeze. Babies also sneeze a lot—it is a good reflex because it clears their noses and can expel viruses and dust. Some babies hiccup a lot, which is also normal. In fact, many babies hiccup in utero. If he hiccuped on the inside, more than likely he will hiccup on the outside, too. Talk to your pediatrician about any concerns and make sure that you understand how babies breathe and eat and poop and sleep. Ask questions, ask questions, ask questions.

Before you leave the hospital, make sure you understand all that you can about your baby. Take advantage of the lactation consultant if your hospital has one or a baby-care information class. The more you know before you leave the hospital, the better prepared you will be before you go home.

Summary

Learn all that you can about the way your baby is going to be born. Learn everything that you can to avoid being separated from your baby. Learn about hospital policies, your doctor's attitudes, what is going to go on during the first few minutes and hours of your baby's life.

CHAPTER THREE

The First Pediatrician Visit

After a baby is born I go to the hospital, reintroduce myself to the parents and meet the baby for the very first time. By now, the parents have been with their baby for an hour or two, or even half a day. Sometimes, if my workday is running long I won't get to see the baby until early evening. So I often speak to the parents on the phone to answer any questions in advance of my visit. They may already have spoken to my office nurse or my lactation consultant.

When I see a baby for the first time I go over him from head to toe, and then give the parents a "guided tour" of their newborn. While you are reading this chapter, take a look at your brand-new baby.

Head

Delivery changes the shape of a baby's head. Babies come out with what many people unkindly call a "cone head." The head can be very pointed because the bones of the skull may have moved around to allow the baby to travel through the birth canal. A baby is born with the skull in separate pieces because of the flexibility required for birth and the flexibility required for the most amazing growth of their lives. I've seen parents who were actually frightened by the appearance of their newborn baby's head because it came to a distinct point and was very swollen. This swelling is due to the pressure of being in the birth canal and being up against the pelvic bones for a long time. It is normal. The head reshapes itself over the first hours and days of life.

At the top and front of the baby's head is the anterior fontanelle, which is diamond shaped and often called the "soft spot." The baby's fontanelle is not as delicate as our mothers led us to believe. You cannot hurt your baby by feeling its fontanelle. If you go back from the front of the baby's head to the posterior fontanelle, you will find a much smaller soft spot that closes over in the first week or two after birth. The anterior fontanelle can stay open for as long as a year or two. If you feel your baby's head you will sometimes feel little bumps on the back of the head, like little developmental cysts. These are all normal. Babies can be born with a little bruise, called a *cephalohematoma*, which can result from the baby bumping its head into the pelvic bones. As that bruise heals over the first few weeks of life, it actually can calcify and feel like a rock or a little volcanic eruption on the baby's head. It is normal, but talk to your doctor about this and have him look closely to reassure you.

Many babies are born with a nice head of hair. Your baby's hair might fall out in the first two or three months. It usually grows back so quickly that you don't notice it, but don't worry if she's bald at three months of age. She'll have lots of hair eventually.

Eyes

Your baby can see only about a foot—far enough to see Mom and Dad. When you look at your baby's eyes you can see that the eye muscles do not work well. Your baby has six eye muscles, one on each side of the eyeball, one at the top, one at the bottom and two corner muscles. They work a little bit. If you are very close to your baby, within a foot, and if you are a very important person in his life and you move very slowly, your baby will watch you. You may see one eye go all the way to the left and the other go all the way to the right but this is normal.

Ears

Your baby has pretty good hearing during the first couple of months and one of the cutest things to see is your baby respond to your voice. He knows your voice because he has been listening to you for six, eight, or ten weeks and will pay close attention when he hears you speak. Your baby's ears are very important to look at because embryologically the ears are taking shape at the same time as the heart and kidneys. A deformed ear is a tip-off to a potential problem. This observation is kind of a crossover from Eastern to Western medicine. Some Eastern medical systems think about the ears as a reflection of the kidneys and heart, and in Western medicine they really are. Your baby most likely has perfect ears and a little minor asymmetry is nothing to worry about. Any type of major ear problem is very noticeable, and if your baby is born with deformities of the ear, your doctor must think about the possibility of deformities of the kidneys or heart and do an ultrasound and other studies.

Nose

Your baby's nose is cute. Babies' noses are meant to be "squished" into the breast, not kept away from the breast. As you can see, the nose actually opens up when you push on it. Your baby can nurse and cuddle into the breast and you do not need to worry. Any species that suffocated while nursing would have been an evolutionary dead end and would have disappeared long ago.

Mouth

Your baby will have a nice strong mouth. If you look at your baby's lips after she comes off the breast, you can see that they are a little swollen. In her lips is a layer of special erectile tissue that is very similar to the tissue on the male penis. This lip tissue becomes very engorged and filled with blood, allowing the baby to latch on. Sometimes this enlarged tissue on the upper lip is called a *nursing blister*. Your baby's jaw will temporarily recede and some people may worry that the baby will not have a good chin line. Don't worry. This is called *relative retrognathia*, which means that the baby's jaw recedes during the first five or six months and sometimes takes a whole year to "pop out" and look just right. This recession of the jaw is a very efficient adaptation as it gets the jaw out of the way for breast-feeding.

Lungs

All babies breathe funny. If you listen closely you'll hear a little panting noise, a little bit of a catch, and sometimes there is a pause for three to five seconds. Babies breathe in irregular patterns and it is normal. It is not unusual for a baby to breathe faster than "normal." Most of my textbooks during medical school and residency taught me that a baby's respiratory pattern should be twenty to thirty times a minute, but a normal baby can breathe forty to fifty times a minute during the first couple of days and it is not worrisome.

Heart

Your baby's heartbeat is fast at two hundred beats per minute. If your baby is excited or angry or even when she is sound asleep, her pulse will not drop below 120 beats per minute throughout the first year of life.

Rib Cage

You can feel your baby's rib cage. If you look at the breastbone you can see it comes in three parts. There is a little notch at the top, then the middle part, and at the very bottom of the breastbone right above the belly button is a little area that almost feels like an arrowhead. The sternum may not fuse to the rest of the breastbone for ten or fifteen years and occasionally will point straight up into the air. You might look at your baby's belly and it might look as if there is a little lump there. This is normal.

Belly Button

The umbilical cord remnant will fall off in one to four weeks and when it does you may see a few drops of blood. There are three scabs from the two arteries and one vein inside the umbilical cord that connected your baby to you. Those little scabs can bleed throughout the first few weeks, and even beyond that you may see a few drops of blood.

Genitals

All baby girls have a vaginal mucus discharge for a month or more. About half of baby girls have a few drops of blood in the diaper on day two or three. This is normal and part of large hormonal changes.

A baby boy's urine by day two or three can get very concentrated—almost granular—and dark orange in appearance, and will look like blood in the diaper. Babies are meant to have very little fluid intake while waiting two to three days for Mom's milk. There is normal swelling of the scrotum. There can be a little bit of extra fluid on one side of the sac. Very rarely there may be a hernia, which your doctor will discuss with you. Occasionally one of the testicles has not come down. It can be higher up in the canal and the doctor can move it down into the scrotal sac. Or, there can be an undescended testicle, which needs to be discussed with your doctor. This rarely requires surgery later in life and your child will be normal, but talk to your doctor about it. Babies who are born prematurely have a much higher incidence of undescended testicles or testicles that retract very easily. Babies who are born breech have a much higher incidence of swollen genitals, whether it's a vagina or penis and testicles. I show parents the two testicles and the penis, which, at this point, is probably uncircumcised no matter what the parents' future plans are. Baby boys (and baby girls) can have some swelling for two reasons: from the pressure of being pressed up against the birth canal and hormonal influences.

CIRCUMCISION

Circumcision for nonreligious reasons is an American tradition. This is the only country, outside of Israel, where circumcision is done at a rate higher than 7 or 8 percent. In Europe, Asia, and other countries, they do not do routine circumcision. While in many cases it is done for religious reasons, in others it is done because it's "always been done that way."

You should know that there are no significant medical benefits of circumcision. There is not an increased risk of cancer of the penis or a partner's cervix or a risk for more infections. Despite what some people say, you should also know that circumcision is not the worst mutilation in the world, either.

Many people say that they want to circumcise their son so that "he will look like Dad." Unless he is a mighty strange-looking baby, he is not going to look like Dad for quite some time! When he is age thirteen or fourteen you can explain that you decided not to circumcise him so as not to take that choice away from him. If he chooses to be circumcised later in life he can do so.

If your son is not circumcised, read a little bit about the intact foreskin. You do not need to retract the foreskin or pull on it. The foreskin is fused to the head of the penis, which is called the *glans penis*, by cells which break down naturally over the first one to thirteen years of a boy's life and allow for sliding and retraction. A fair number of one-year-old baby boys have foreskins that retract while others do not. While there are still some doctors who think that the foreskin should be retracted forcibly, don't push it and don't force it. Allow the foreskin to retract at its own pace. Some boys' foreskins do not retract until puberty. As long as the penis looks okay, and as long as your baby is having erections that are not terribly uncomfortable, and as long as he can urinate a clear stream then you do not need to do anything to the foreskin except leave it alone.

In my opinion, circumcision is not the best thing for the baby, and if you can avoid circumcising your son, do so. If you choose circumcision, make sure the person doing it is very good at it and uses anesthesia of some kind—topical or local. Whatever your choice, it is not wrong. It is a personal choice that is dependent on your personal and religious views.

URINATION

Your baby will not urinate much in the first two days, maybe only once or twice during the first day. They become little water conservationists while waiting for Mom's milk to come in. Your baby's urine will become very scanty and dark for a few days. This is normal. A baby who is getting a high level of breast milk will urinate anywhere from two to five times an hour, up to one hundred times a day. The diaper will be perceived as wet eight to ten times a day. It is actually a lot wetter than that. Babies who have a drop in urine output need a lot of extra observation because it's usually inadequate between the baby and the breast-feeding mom and needs lactation consultation and help. The baby almost never needs supplementation, certainly not with water, almost never with formula and rarely with pumped breast milk. Instead, the breast-feeding relationship needs to be evaluated by an expert and helped. Decreased output of urine during illness during the first two to six months of life requires a call to your doctor.

Legs, Hands, and Feet

Breech babies can be born with very funny-looking legs. The feet can be all the way up behind their ears and they may not unfold for hours or days. If you look at your baby's quadriceps they tend to be huge and bulky because the baby earned them by kicking Mommy as hard as he or she could during the pregnancy and labor. If your baby's legs look bulky during the first year that is normal.

I always feel your baby's pulses in the groin area and in other places. I also check your baby's hips because occasionally, but rarely, babies are born with hips that easily dislocate. This occurs in one out of one hundred babies or so. I check for this by moving your baby's hips around. I extend the legs and push down a little bit to see whether or not the hip socket is too shallow. If it is, the earlier this is diagnosed the better.

If a hip dislocation is found on your baby during the examination by your pediatrician, the pediatrician will refer you to an orthopedist for an ultrasound or X ray. Some babies just need to be double diapered to spread their legs a little bit and to push the hip bone into the socket to make the socket deeper. Other babies need a brace. If so, your doctor will refer you to an orthopedic surgeon.

Your baby's hands and feet will get cold and blue during the first six to twelve months, not because of ambient temperature, but because the arteries go into spasm. You can have twenty booties on your baby's feet and they will still be blue underneath the booties. Don't bother overdressing, but dress your baby for simple comfort. During the first week you can add a light blanket, but after the first week don't bother. Babies who are overwrapped get hot and sweaty, get rashes, and don't eat well. Babies are better off at sixty-five degrees with a nice little shirt on than they are at seventy-five degrees. Hot, dry air is just not good for them.

Babies do better in cool, moist air. Hot, dry air isn't good for their eyes, nose, throat, or lungs. I tell moms and dads to keep the windows open when possible and to keep the heat off whenever possible if the temperature is reasonable. Obviously, you can't keep your windows open in January in the Midwest if it is ten degrees out. You'll have to make some compromises. The heat will have to be on, but keep a cool mister humidifer going. Cool mist is the best thing for a baby's nose, throat, and lungs. In the hospital if a baby gets really sick and has respiratory difficulties, the oxygen delivered is always humidified and some babies are actually put in a cool-mist tent.

Skin

Your baby will get lots of little rashes, little plugged ducts on her nose, and little red splotches on day two or three. These splotches are misnamed *erythema toxin* although they are not toxins and they probably have more to do with hormonal changes. They tend to look like fleabites—little red splotches with a little white dot in the middle. Newborn acne can start at any time in the first week or two and can last for a long time. Babies also tend to get little cracks and peels around their ankles and wrists. Eventually they shed all of that old skin. Sometimes it is noticeable, sometimes not. It is all normal.

Babies can also be born with many different types of birthmarks. The most common birthmarks are the little "stork bites," which are little red splotches on the back of the neck, and "angel kisses," which are little red splotches on the eyelids. They are an extra collection of blood vessels in very thin skin. Eighty or 90 percent of them disappear within the first few years of life. Other types of birthmarks are capillary hemangiomas or "strawberry marks," which can occur on the arm or belly and occasionally on the cheek. Discuss this with your doctor because some of these marks actually need to be treated early in life with laser treatment. Most of them do not. Seventy to 90 percent are gone by kindergarten. But, if the mark is on the cheek you may want to have something done prior to preschool.

Summary

Schedule the first pediatrician visit at two weeks of age. I also schedule a house call for my lactation consultant and tell parents to please feel free to call my office to speak to me, to one of my nurses, or to my lactation consultant any time during the first two weeks. By that first visit, however, most parents have a long list of questions. I urge you to write those questions down and to make sure there will be plenty of time at the first pediatrician visit to talk about everything you'd like to know. You'll want to make sure you are prepared for the next couple of months because you won't see your doctor again until the baby is about two months of age. During the visit ask about everything that is troubling you, make sure your doctor makes a nice contact with you and your baby, and make sure that before your doctor walks out the door, all of your questions have been answered.

CHAPTER FOUR

The Care and Feeding of Your Baby

The philosophy involved in the first week or two, or year or two, is very simple. Your baby talks and you listen. Everybody attempts to complicate the story. They imply that you might spoil your baby and should not pick him up so much or let him eat so much. I tell the parents you cannot overfeed or over-hug a baby. You can spoil a three-year-old when she whines and you give her cookies. Then she learns to whine and cry for a cookie. When your baby cries, it is her highest and virtually only level of communication.

As a new parent you are dealing with your baby's most basic human and physiologic needs—hunger, warmth, trust, and cuddles. If you say to your baby, "You know, we're not going to feed you until it is three and it is only ten minutes till three," the feeling you engender in your baby is that she is not as important as she thinks she is and you are not as smart as you look. What you want to say is, "I want you to say what you want and when you want it (even though it is unbelievable that you actually want more because you just had some)." By doing this, you allow the baby to control whatever is important to her life. When your child reaches twelve months, all you need to do is adjust her pedestal from ten feet to nine.

Psychologists do a good job of talking about external personalities and internal personalities. The external is when you wake up and think, "I wonder what's going to happen to me today?" The internal is when you wake up and think, "I wonder what I should make happen today?" I am convinced this all begins right at birth. Shortly after birth we say to a baby, "What do you need? What do you want? You are in charge in whatever is important to you." And then toward the baby's ninth, tenth, or twelfth month we have to back off a little bit, and what this says to the baby is that you are now in charge of the things that you need in your environment. All of your needs will be met, but you make things happen. And then later, when we have made this baby feel incredibly powerful and incredibly special, we say, you know, we are also very special people and there will be times when you're going to have to wait a minute. I think a lot of the basis of American child rearing gets this upside down.

During those first few hours and first few days, I talk to parents about the fact that you cannot really over-hug your baby. Nobody gets over-hugged. Very few people get overloved and yet that is what a lot of pop parenting "experts" will imply because they may recommend limiting your baby's hugs. When your baby has a certain look on his face and your baby is crying, you need to respond. It's not always likely that the baby is saying, "Gee, I'm tired, find me a place to sleep." Your baby is saying, "Hug me! Change whatever is going on! If I'm wet, please get me dry. If I'm hungry, please feed me. If I'm alone, please pick me up." There are books that tell you to offer your baby sleep when he is tired just as you would offer your baby food when he is hungry. Sleep discussions which put together clever acronyms, clever phrases about offering sleep and so on, may be clever but not accurate. I think these are very clever things to say: Offer your baby sleep as you offer food when it's hungry, but I don't think it's accurate to always assume a baby who looks a little out of sorts is sleepy. The baby might actually be hungry, might actually be wet, might actually need to be hugged or taken for a walk around the block. I do agree that it is a good idea to get in touch with your baby's sleep rhythms as best as you can, but realize these sleep rhythms are not set in stone and that, therefore, they change and, therefore, parents have to be flexible.

Sleep

In America what we have done for years and what is encouraged by a lot of parenting books is to take the power away from the baby. In some ways it is easier to say to parents, "You know, the baby needs to soothe himself to sleep and you need to take back part of your life . . ." and so on. If your goal is to get more sleep this year, then you have made a mistake by having a baby. You may get six hours a night, but it won't be consecutive because babies don't sleep like that. Adults go through sleep cycles every three hours from a shallow period of sleep, down to deep and back up to shallow. Babies can cycle every hour or so. Therefore, there is a volatile period during almost every hour. So if a baby gets a little gas bubble or if a dog barks next door the baby wakes up.

I do not recommend separate sleeping quarters for your baby. There has been some controversy over babies sleeping with parents, but scientists and experts on babies' sleep maintain that the safest place for babies to sleep is either right next to you or very close by. A separate room for your baby is not advisable and probably not even safe. Your baby is born somewhat unstable and breathes funny. The heartbeat and respiratory patterns are synchronized to the mother for nine months. Now that the baby is out and getting hugged by two people, her patterns can synchronize to two people. It is not scientifically sound and it's not safe to separate a baby and her parents during the first six to twelve months of life. I recommend either sleeping with her in the same bed or with your little co-sleeper right next to your bed, or, at the very least, a little bassinet a foot or two away.

It is much easier to attend to your baby's needs when you have the baby in bed with you. You will not hurt your baby or roll over on your baby. If you roll over on him, he will lift his elbow and hit you in the ribs.

The Power of the Breast

I see some people who aren't quite sure exactly how they want to raise their babies. They've heard, of course, that breast-feeding is the best way to go and that there are some advantages to the family bed, but they're confused and they come to me for advice. I give the best advice I can, based on everything I have learned and read as well as on twenty-two years' worth of experience. I believe in choice. I believe that people have a right to have a baby or not to have a baby. I think you have a right to have two or three or twelve children. But once you decide you want to have a baby, I think you should set out to raise the baby in the best way possible. I tell parents, unequivocally, that breast-feeding is the indisputable cornerstone of good health for babies.

The benefits of breast-feeding are incalculable. Babies who are breast-fed get fewer infections, grow just the way they are supposed to grow, and gain as much weight as they are supposed to gain. They remain on a continuum of that nine months within the womb where the baby was built out of an ultra-filtered bloodstream where the blood filtered through the placenta. Babies should continue on the outside for another three to twenty months breast-feeding, again eating an ultra-filtrate of the bloodstream. When Mom produces the milk, babies are healthier.

On average, babies who are breast-fed have an IQ that is approximately eight points higher than those who are not. There are probably at least two hundred pieces of medical literature that show that a baby who is breast-fed develops fine motor skills, gross motor skills, and cognitive skills more quickly than non-breast-fed babies. Also, the retina is completely different in a breast-fed baby, and the visual cortex develops differently in a baby who is breast-fed. The retina is the crucial receptive part of the eyeball and it is very special. It's been shown that in the breast-fed baby the retina develops differently because the constituents of breast milk are exactly what the retina needs to develop. There are certain amino acids which are not found in the same balance in artificial foods and formula.

During the first six months or so of life the baby's intestines are a microscopic latticework and large proteins can leak through. So if a baby's intestines are challenged with soy-milk formula or with cow's-milk formula, these proteins are big allergenic proteins that can leak through the intestines, get into the bloodstream, and trigger an immune response, which can lead to many more allergies and a lot more eczema and asthma. In a family where there is a history of allergies, breast-feeding is crucial. It's not much less crucial in a family without allergies because allergies can occur for the first time in a family in this way. Breast-feeding is the solution to preventing allergies.

There are a lot of personal choices to be made when you are pregnant and when you actually have your baby. Whether or not to breast-feed is very much a medical discussion between the doctor and the parents. It is not the personal choice, as some people would have you believe. It is a medical issue. Moms who breast-feed their babies have children with fewer ear infections and allergies, less pneumonia and diarrhea; they also get well sooner if they do get sick and are easier to treat. I can go through weeks and even months without seeing a breast-fed baby younger than six months of age with an ear infection. Babies who are breast-fed also have less cancer as teenagers, and the intestinal bacteria is set up just right. Not only is breast milk the perfect food for babies, moms who breast-feed for six months or longer have been shown to have a 50 percent decrease in breast cancer and a 30 to 40 percent decrease in thyroid cancer, since breast-feeding synchronizes the body's hormonal system.

Breast milk is a living fluid that is made by Mom each day. It contains antibodies against whatever viruses are around. Your baby drinks these antibodies, then the antibodies make it into your baby's bloodstream and your baby is protected. This is called *enteromammary circulation* and it works like this: Mom kisses Dad's forehead, taking the virus off his forehead, processes it through her mature immune system, and develops antibodies to the virus. The antibodies then get into her bloodstream and her milk, which the baby ingests, which protects baby from Dad's cold. It's almost like magic.

In addition to the health benefits of breast-feeding your baby, there are practical reasons, too. For one, babies who are breast-fed are more portable. If you are formula feeding your baby and you want to take a trip to visit your relatives or if you want to take a trip to France, you have to bring formula with you or be sure they have the right kind of formula available. You have to bring bottles and a little cooler and make sure the water is safe. You will have to deal with a lot more spit up, and the baby (and you, too!) will smell funny on the airplane. But, if you are breast-feeding your baby and you want to go to France or New Mexico on the spur of the moment you are set to go. Some people look at breast-feeding as something that will tie them down, when instead, it liberates them from needing refrigeration and convenience stores.

If you come to my office and say, "You know, breast-feeding just isn't for me. I really don't know if I want to spend that much time with the baby, and I'd really like to get back to my life," I would suggest that you reconsider if you want a child in your life at this time. If you come to my office and say, "I intend to raise my baby in the second or third best way possible," and you want me to work as hard as I can as your baby's doctor, I would have to tell you that I don't think we would get along.

I suggest that once you decide you are going to have a baby you figure out how to build enough flexibility into your life so you can raise the baby in the best way you can. This involves having the healthiest pre-pregnancy period, the healthiest pregnancy, seeking out the healthiest and best birth for you and your family, and breast-feeding your baby from day one and giving your baby nothing but breast milk. There is no question in the medical or parents' community about whether or not breast-feeding is the best thing for a baby.

Some doctors tell me that the reason they don't push breast-feeding is that mothers feel guilty. I recently had a mother tell me that my advice made her feel guilty, so I explained to her that the guilt I more commonly see is when the child is a year or two old and a mom comes to me and complains. The mom usually says, "I feel so guilty that I didn't know what I know now about breast-feeding, or about hugging my baby more. I feel guilty and a little bit angry at you for not telling me my baby would get more ear infections, was at higher risk for getting pneumonia or respiratory syncitial virus (RSV), or other viruses if I didn't breast-feed. I feel bad and guilty and a little bit angry that I did not get more advice and support about helping me breast-feed my baby, more guidance regarding the family bed, and so-called attachment parenting, 'wearing' my baby everywhere I go, hugging my baby, and devoting all this time and energy to the baby." (RSV is a virus that comes every winter. It inflames the airways from the throat to the lungs. It creates swelling, a lot of extra mucus, and can endanger a young baby, especially a baby in the first five to seven months of life, or a baby who was born prematurely and therefore has a lot more sensitive airways. RSV is very, very common, and breast milk seems to protect a baby against RSV better than artificial food does.)

Babies take a lot of time and attention. One of the analogies I draw for people is to imagine that nine months ago you opened a little flower shop. You have to get up at four in the morning to go to the market to buy the flowers and then you work behind the counter all day long. You work until closing and after closing you have to do the books yourself since you don't have a bookkeeper. You may get to bed at ten o'clock in the evening, but you are up again at four to start all over again. Over the course of nine or twelve months you've made a success of the flower shop and people are saying, "Wow! This is incredible. You have put every minute of every day into that flower shop and it's almost making a profit."

Now, imagine you have a nine-month-old baby and it's the nicest, sweetest, healthiest nine-month-old baby. People will say things like, "If we knew we could have one like this then we'd have a baby." At the same time they'll say, "We haven't seen you! What have you been doing? You're doing nothing but spending time with that baby! You haven't even been to lunch, you haven't taken tennis lessons, you don't go out, we haven't seen you and your husband for dinner." Somehow they think your great baby is great by accident or genetics and not about the time and energy you've devoted to her care and well-being. If you put all your time into the flower shop it's okay, but if you put all your time into the baby it's seen as taking time from everything else. I am here to tell you: Put the time into the baby. It will be well worth it. You will raise a happy, healthy child.

As I've mentioned previously, breast-feeding is one of the cornerstones to raising a happy, healthy child. Breast-feeding seems to go in and out of vogue. In the early part of the twentieth century, doctors decided to take a little more control over the feeding of the baby and developed formulas. They instructed mothers on how much concentrated milk and how much sugar and/or Karo syrup and other artificial ingredients to use. Doctors implied that Mom's breast milk was either not good enough, modern enough, or might not be nourishing enough to produce wellness. This is particularly true in America. If you lived almost anywhere else at any other time, you would have watched your mother breast-feeding your siblings and your aunt breast-feeding your cousins. You would have seen breast-feeding mothers in your community. Today, you can become an adult in America and know nothing about breast-feeding. But you can learn.

Let me be clear. There are very, very few women who cannot breast-feed. Your milk flows. The hormones are all set up. Colostrum, the pre-milk, flows first. It's a little thicker and very heavy in antibodies, and it only flows in small amounts. A baby who is breast-feeding perfectly for the first two days is going to get only two or three teaspoons of colostrum. Many hospitals do not seem to understand this and they imply that there is not enough milk and the baby is going to go hungry. Babies who get a warm bottle of formula in the nursery have an increased tendency to get allergies—even from one bottle. So make sure the hospital knows you are a breast-feeding family and that you do not want them to give your baby any formula or bottles of anything. Remember that babies are not that fragile. A baby has an extra pound of water and fat and can get by on only breast milk. If you give a baby water, the water fills the baby up, the baby does not nurse as well, does not suck as strong, and then the milk comes in late. The mother goes home from the hospital with a baby who has not learned how to suck and now you have problems. The easiest way to avoid these problems is to keep your baby with you at all times.

Even if breast-feeding comes naturally to you, it is very helpful to have someone coach you and show you exactly where your elbow should go to help support you. It does require practice. It is like any other physical activity, like learning how to hit a backhand in tennis. The first few back-hands aren't so great. The first time that you breast-feed may not be so easy. You must be patient and persistent. A baby is not endangered if breast-feeding does not go well during the first day or two.

Possible Breast-Feeding Challenges

Inverted nipples (when a woman's nipples don't stand out when the baby nurses) may need a little extra attention. Sometimes they need to be drawn out by a breast pump. Moms need to know techniques for moving their nipples around to get them out so that the baby can breast-feed. The more common problem involves latch-on—getting the baby lined up, getting the baby's mouth wide open, tickling the baby's lips with your nipple, and squishing your baby on to your breast so that the nipple ends up in the back of the baby's throat. You must also learn how to unlatch a baby by breaking suction and getting ahead of any challenges like cracking or bleeding nipples. If nipples become abraded or cracked because of difficult breast-feeding at the beginning, lactation consultation should be done. Lactation consultation is a specialty. A person who has orthopedic problems goes to an orthopedist; a person with skin problems goes to a dermatologist. Lactation problems should not necessarily be treated by your pediatrician or by your obstetrician. You will need somebody skilled and expert and trained in lactation. A lot of women do have a difficult time in America and elsewhere with breast-feeding because we have lost that instinct and because support and information is either lacking or nonexistent.

A home visit from a lactation consultant is easy to set up. There is a website address for the International Board of Lactation Consultants Examiners (www.iblce.org). You can ask in your hospital nursery or call La Leche League of doctors or La Leche International. Your hospital's nursery or doctor can direct you to a lactation consultant. Some of them are good, some are great, some might not be to your liking, but it is important to know where to find one, especially if you need one. I have a lactation consultant in my office who follows up on breast-feeding issues with every mother in the hospital and then during the first day or two they are home. There are lactation consultants in every big and medium-sized community in the United States. Parents should get as much breast-feeding advice as possible because, sadly, we have very successfully eliminated the cultural instinct for breast-feeding over the past couple of generations. Even though it will go well for most people, it is helpful to be shown where to move your elbow and get some coaching about breast-feeding.

An adopted baby can also be breast-fed. A mom who is going to adopt a baby and wants to breast-feed should get a breast pump if possible three months before the baby is to be born. She does not need hormonal injections, but she may want to take certain herbs that promote breast-feeding; but if she pumps her breast three to six times a day, she will get colostrum almost every time. A baby who is adopted may not get a full supply of breast milk, but using the supplementary nursing systems available, an adopted mom can usually breast-feed her baby. Adoption is a special circumstance, and the baby's health and nutrition are the most important considerations; therefore, artificial formulas might be required.

Mothers need to know that babies are meant to enter into a state of relative dehydration right after birth. A baby will lose anywhere from 3 to 10 percent of its birth weight during those first few days. Hunger and thirst will trigger stronger sucking. A mother should put her baby to her breast every hour or two during the day and every two or three during the night, then switch breasts often. The more often a mom switches breasts during the first few days of birth, every five, six, to seven minutes, the sooner her milk comes in and the greater the quantity of milk she gets. An overabundant supply of milk does occur for some moms, especially in week two or three. Decreasing the number of feedings should slow down the milk and may be just what she needs.

Getting Ready to Breast-Feed

A mom who is getting ready to breast-feed should have clean hands. She does not have to wash her breasts or wash her nipples with soap. As a matter of fact, babies find the nipple partially by smell, so you do not want to use any perfumes or perfumed soaps. Moms need to take good care of their breasts, and I tell moms that if they feel that their breasts weigh a hundred pounds each by the end of the first week to get a really good nursing bra. I also encourage them to take a good look at the other accessories available for nursing: pillows and little nursing stools that support feet at just the right angle and help the back. If sore nipples are a problem the solution is proper positioning and proper nursing techniques. Lansinoh creme can help, as well as others that moisturize the nipples and decrease some of the superficial irritation.

Some dads have a little trouble finding a role in American parenting, especially within breast-feeding families. It is not necessary for fathers to give a bottle of expressed milk in the first weeks or months of life. Instead, Dad should be there to support Mom and the new baby. Dad can make sure that Mom is eating instead of trying to feed the baby. Dads can also be involved in parenting by listening closely to their baby. Usually a baby wants Mom to feed him, but Dad can change his diapers, take a bath with him, and take him for a walk. Dad is also needed to hug and comfort the baby. He can also let the baby suck on his well-washed finger.

The only common problem I see with breast-feeding, and the only common challenge, involves getting your baby to latch on. I tell moms to hold their baby in their arms with the baby's bottom in their hand, tucking their baby's head into the crook of the elbow. Have your baby lying on his side, not on his back, so he won't have to turn to get to your breast. If your baby is lying on his side he'll fall into the breast. You can tickle his mouth with your nipple or wait until his mouth is wide open, and then lovingly try to squish him into the breast almost as if you were trying to smother him. You don't have to worry about the baby suffocating at the breast. Their noses are structured so they can get air. You will hear your baby breathing and he will be fine.

If your baby latches on and your nipple hurts, break the suction. Put your finger into your baby's mouth and pop to make sure your baby does not slide off your nipple. If your baby latches on incorrectly it can be like sandpapering your nipple. When your baby is positioned properly he will be latched on to the areola, the large, darker part of the breast surrounding the nipple, and the nipple will "float" in the back of the baby's throat. Nurse your baby for three to five minutes on one side, break suction, switch to the other side, and go back and forth every five or six minutes during the first week. The more often you switch breasts and the more often you nurse, the sooner your milk comes in.

On day two or three the milk supply sometimes gets ahead of the baby and some moms get engorged. What happens is the milk supply is a little higher than the baby can handle and the contour of the breast changes and the baby has a little trouble wrapping his mouth around it. As a result, the mom's breast becomes a little more engorged and the baby has a little more trouble latching on; you can get a bad cycle going. The way to stop the cycle is for the mom to either hand express or pump a little bit of milk, just to soften the contour of the breasts so the baby can latch on. In most cultures, other than America, the father does this job. He expresses a little milk for the mom and softens the breasts for the baby. When I mention this to American moms and dads, some understand and some say, "Ohhhhh." But it is a normal thing to do. If you have trouble with engorgement, get help via phone or in person from a lactation consultant.

Your Breast Milk Is What You Eat

At least half of babies do not like cow's milk coming through Mom's breast milk. Some babies do not like peanuts. Some babies hate it when you eat eggs. All babies like garlic. All babies like it when you eat lots of vegetables. Foods that allegedly cause gas, like broccoli and cabbage and so on, do not cause gas in babies. They may cause gas in the mother but they do not hurt the baby. You may need to change your diet when you are breast-feeding because some babies do not tolerate certain proteins like dairy or eggs or peanuts. They also may have trouble with wheat or citrus. Dairy is usually the biggest culprit for gas or upset stomachs in babies. I've seen some babies who have a few drops of blood in their stools even if Mom had a teaspoon of milk in her tea in the morning. I talked with a mom recently who could not eat eggplant. The baby did great until she ate eggplant and then the baby had blood in the stool. You need to watch what you eat and see how your baby reacts to your diet.

In general, babies are very gassy. Breast-feeding babies are often no less gassy than a baby getting formula. Your breast-fed baby will be gassy, cranky, and sleepless sometimes and may need bouncing. Breast-fed babies do not burp much. They may burp by accident while you are getting them into position to burp but they don't burp much and there is no point in thumping them on the back for ten minutes to get them to burp. Try to burp your baby for about one minute; otherwise give up.

There is a medical condition called *gastroesophageal reflux* or just *reflux*. It's been recognized a lot better in the last ten years or so. Babies with this problem spit up a lot and they have a kind of baby heartburn, which can cause them to be quite cranky all day. This is not a baby who just spits up. This is a baby who spits up constantly, and is a baby who does not smile. Some of these babies need medication and some of them will be cured when Mom changes her diet. All of these babies will be helped if Mom keeps him upright after feeding and burps him more frequently.

There is a band of muscle between the esophagus and the stomach and this is supposed to keep food down in the stom-ach. Babies with reflux, or adults with heartburn, get the bounce of stomach contents and stomach acids from the stomach up into the esophagus and it burns and leads to spitting up. There can be some complications from reflux and these babies need to be looked at closely. If I suspect a baby has bad reflux I send the baby to a pediatric gastroenterologist.

Some Concerns about Breast-Feeding

Many mothers are concerned that they don't have enough breast milk, even when their babies are doing well. Doing well will mean that they are urinating, having bowel movements, eating eagerly, and growing. A baby initially loses anywhere from 3 to 10 percent of body weight in the first few days of life as water is used up and fat metabolizes. A baby who is doing well, as I put it, is eager to eat, eager to go to the breast, starting to urinate, and starting to have bowel movements. A baby who is doing well after the first few weeks is making nice eye contact, has more facial expression, is an eager, vigorous baby with good muscle tone, good skin color, and again, is urinating and having bowel movements.

If the baby is not doing well then I have to take a closer look at him and do a little more of a consultation, but more likely a mom will say, "You know, I am convinced that I don't have enough milk because he is growing well but he wants to eat all the time." If a baby wants to eat and is doing well, then by all means feed him. In fact, if a baby wants to eat all the time, it's because you have lots of milk, which is the opposite of what people would lead you to believe. In the first year of life, a baby is eating. There is no "he just ate." He may take an hour or two off, but he is always eating. He will double his weight in four or five months and triple his weight in the first year of life, and he needs a lot of calories to do so. And Mom is the restaurant, waiter, and waitress all in one. It's hard work but the rewards are great.

Breast-fed babies tend to lose some weight and regain it anywhere from two to three weeks of age. It's not unusual in my practice to see a baby at the two-week check-up a few ounces under birth weight. This is normal. Some breast-feeding babies regain birth weight at three weeks of age. Weight loss or slow weight gain is not a reason to supplement the baby or worry or get tests. It is an indication to watch the mom breast-feed and to help her as much as she needs.

It took me many years to go from *saying* I wasn't worried about a baby being under birth weight to actually *not* being worried about a baby being under birth weight. A baby who looks good, is nursing strongly, and is urinating and having bowel movements at two weeks of age but is still a few ounces under birth weight is not a worrisome baby. I might bring the baby in for an extra visit to check the weight. I might ask the lactation consultant to watch the mom nurse and help her, or I might do it myself.

Babies get hungry every one to three hours. You might be sitting at home in a nice quiet room by yourself or with your family, or you might be out shopping or in a restaurant and your baby will get hungry and need to eat. There is nothing wrong, and everything right, about breast-feeding in public.

There are laws that protect the right of women to nurse in public. Many moms want to nurse in public but also want to be discreet and there are many ways to do this, such as using a shawl or blanket. In addition there are many styles of nursing tops that have flaps or other openings that allow you to nurse comfortably. Again, you can exercise your personal choice about how, or if, you will nurse in public.

American culture has turned the breast into a sexual symbol. We are the only culture that looks at breasts this way. Popular movies, magazines, television and so on are responsible for this. Breasts are meant to feed babies. I can't say it too many times: Breasts are meant to feed babies. A year or two of breast-feeding is very, very good for babies. Babies who are breast-fed longer than that are just fine.

Some babies go through growth spurts during the first week or so. Your baby may want to eat all day and night. I will get a frantic phone call, "He cries until I feed him." The solution is pretty obvious but may not be so obvious at three in the morning: Feed him and he won't cry. The real answer is you cannot overfeed him. Let me repeat: You cannot overfeed a breast-feeding baby. Better to feed the baby than use a pacifier. Pacifiers increase the incidence of ear infection, probably because they decrease the success of breast-feeding. Especially between the first week or two, pacifiers focus on how to keep the baby quiet, rather than what the baby needs. Babies' cries are the highest level of communication they have and the best response that most moms can have is to feed them. You can't overfeed your baby. There may be times when you may want to walk your baby, bounce your baby a little bit, or sing to your baby, and maybe that's what your baby needs right at that time, but almost every time a baby cries, she needs to be picked up and fed, especially during the first weeks of life. You can't overfeed a baby if you are breast-feeding.

In fact, babies are pretty good at knowing just how much to eat. I tell parents at the two-week check-up that their baby has a little computer above those cute little eyebrows and if that computer reads seven pounds, nine ounces on June 28, it means that the baby will weigh exactly what she is supposed to weigh. No more, no less. If you try to underfeed a baby or if you unbutton your blouse too slowly, the baby yells. If your baby overfeeds himself because it was so good, he will probably spit up because he is supposed to weigh exactly this amount today. Adults will compensate for eating too much one day by attempting to fast the next day. Babies never do that. They eat exactly the right amount of calories every day. Babies gain weight the way they are supposed to gain weight. Some babies gain very slowly. There are growth charts that were developed using data from formula-fed babies in the twenties, thirties, forties, and fifties that are in no way applicable to your twenty-first-century baby. Babies should write growth charts—not follow them. I have never helped a baby with a growth chart. I have never said to a parent, "Gee, your baby looks great, but the growth chart looks like hell, so we need to do something." A baby grows at the pace that suits him.

Some babies get big quickly. Often, they have big parents. Some babies grow very slowly and they don't double their weight in the first four or five months like an "average" baby does. They grow slowly and they are perfectly healthy. The numbers matter a lot less than the baby. What I tell parents is that we need to look at the *baby* not how the baby is on the scale since the scale does not really give useful information on a baby who is doing great.

You don't need to limit feeding a baby who is growing fast and you don't need to supplement breast-feeding babies who are growing slowly. I will look and make sure things are going well and ask questions such as, Is the breast-feeding going well, with eagerness and lack of pain? How is the urine output and stooling? But a baby who is playing, peeing, pooping, growing, and hitting her developmental milestones (smiling at two months, laughing at four, and nearly sitting at six) does not need any tests or supplements while breast-feeding. Doctors sometimes become nervous about breast-fed babies because they cannot measure how much milk the baby is getting. I think we need to look less at numbers and look at how the baby is doing. By the time a baby approaches his first birthday, it will be pretty obvious that the baby is going to meet the genetics of their parents.

For parents who are concerned about slow growth in their baby let me tell you that in twenty-two years of practice I have never seen slow growth in a baby as the only sign of something bad going on. I have seen babies who have some bad problems like lung or heart problems or neurological system problems, but these babies have had more wrong with them than just growing slowly. Every baby I have seen who has grown slowly was okay.

Babies also know how often they need to eat. Rigidly scheduling your baby does not make sense. If you think about your baby's blood-sugar pattern while in utero, the blood-sugar pattern is just flat, all day and all night. Your baby has the exact same amount of blood sugar, the same amount of fuel building your baby. An adult's blood-sugar pattern looks like a roller coaster. It goes up and down throughout the day. Once a baby is born, its blood-sugar pattern is very jagged. Your baby can eat for an hour straight, take three minutes off and come right back and eat as if he has not eaten for hours. Because your baby is growing fast, your baby can be hungry all day. This is because there is a lot of activity going on inside your baby. His metabolic rate is higher and his furnace is really going so you want to keep him growing and keep him warm so the blood sugar can rise and drop normally. The bottom line: Feed him on demand.

Hug Your Baby

People may tell you or imply that feeding on demand means feeding him too much or that picking him up too often is not good. They are wrong. As an example, I will tell you my favorite story about a mom with a two-week-old baby who transferred to me after seeing another doctor. She had taken her baby to her two-week check-up and the doctor had looked her right in the eye and said, "If you pick her up and feed her every time she cries, she's going to think she can get you whenever she needs you." The mother said, "She *can* get me whenever she needs me." Then she transferred her baby's care to me because I agreed with her point of view.

Babies in the first weeks or months always need to be hugged and fed, and you cannot spoil them. By attending to their needs you have set up a foundation of love, warmth, and trust that you can build on later.

Babies who are raised in a so-called attachment way, where parents hug and cuddle as much as possible, separate easier later on because their foundation of trust is so strong. Babies know when they are loved and respected. Some "experts" claim they will show you how to respect your baby and then turn around and teach you how to disrespect her. They will tell you that when the baby cries you need to stretch things out a bit and that some babies need to cry. The cliché that "crying is good for a baby's lungs" is just not true.

Babies cry for a reason. It is how they communicate and tell Mom and Dad if they are hungry or wet. A crying baby is a talking baby. Listening closely to your baby is one of the lost arts of parenting. If you listen to your baby she will tell you what she needs at all times. Babies never cry without a reason. I get parents who will call and say, "Every time I put her down, she starts to cry." Well, I think the solution is obvious, but I ask, "What happens when you pick her up?" Invariably they say, "When I pick her up, she stops crying." Clearly this is a baby who wants to be picked up. Babies don't like being put down. They are not separate from their mothers during the nine months in utero and babies do not like being separate from their mommies and daddies during the first few weeks or months outside.

Colic

Babies do get colic or become colicky. Colic is a medical condition without a known cause. We aren't even sure what colic is. We do know that babies who have colic will cry for three to five hours and nothing you do will stop it. Babies with colic tend to become adults with irritable intestines. Unfortunately, many babies who are labeled as being "colicky" are just babies who are communicating and not being heard. Their parents may have been told not to feed the baby often or pick up the baby every time he cries. But, the baby will just keep crying because he has something to say and no one is listening to him.

Baths

Baths are a lot of fun and babies like them and so do parents. However, a lot of parents overclean their babies. There is good new evidence that a little bit of dirt is good for us since it helps to build our immune systems. If we stay too clean and do not play outside enough, our immune system is not exposed to enough dirt or enough germs and it does not develop well. This is not an endorsement for your baby to go out into the garden and eat dirt, which babies tend to do, but it is an encouragement to allow your baby to get dirty and not to overbathe.

Babies do not need baths every day and do not need long baths because bathing dries out their skin. Children with skin problems, especially eczema, should have as few baths as possible. I think that bath time is Daddy's time and think it is great if the baby gets in the tub with Daddy for a nice bath. In some ways, babies are like cold-blooded animals in that in cold water, they will cool down, and in hot water they will heat up. Their core is very close to the surface. So a bath that is over one hundred degrees is not good for a baby. The temperature of the water should be as close to body temperature as possible.

A Matter of Perspective

About six or seven years ago I was doing two-week check-ups for two different babies. In one room was a baby who weighed about seven pounds at birth and gained about four ounces since then. This told me that the baby was gaining weight and looked good. I then looked at the parents—they looked like they were dying. They were tired and they looked exhausted. They said, "What are we going to do? This baby wakes up every hour or two and eats and eats all through the night and we are getting no sleep!" Because the baby was gaining weight and looking good I tried to reassure the parents the best I could that all was as it should be, but it was a hard visit.

In the next room was a two-week old baby who was born at about seven pounds and had gained nine ounces. I noticed on the chart that the nurse had noted that the baby sleeps through the night. I thought this was interesting and said, "Your baby is gaining weight and doing nicely, and he's also sleeping through the night. Is he breast-feeding or are you supplementing?" They told me they were just feeding the baby breast milk. I pressed them a little since it is unusual for a baby at that age to sleep through the night. And they said, "Yes, he sleeps right through the night. He wakes up every hour or two to eat but sleeps through the night."

I realized then that a lot of parenting and other things

with babies are perceptual. These babies were eating, growing, and behaving the same. The baby in room one was up
every hour to nurse and the parents were fighting it all the
way. (Probably because a well-meaning someone had told
them a baby can't nurse all night long). So the parents felt
there was something wrong. The parents in room two
understood they had a baby who was growing rapidly and
that they were going to be up feeding him. Their perception
was that their baby was sleeping through the night (even
though he had the same eating pattern as baby number one)
because they adapted themselves to their baby's pattern and
didn't fight it.

CHAPTER FIVE

Two Days, Two Weeks, Two Months

The first two weeks at home after your baby's birth can be the most difficult because you have to figure out, first, which end of the baby is up, and then you have to figure out how to deal with a boss who pushes you around a lot more than any other boss ever has. You have never—and will never—work for anyone who awakens you at one, three, then five in the morning and makes demands on your time and energy. The first two weeks can be tricky. I recommend that you just go along with it. Don't fight what has to be done. If you acquiesce to the baby's needs you will realize that this is a brand-new wonderful job with rewards that are commensurate with the amount of work you put into it—very unlike almost any other job you have done in your life.

No one can really prepare you for the first two weeks at home. As you know by now, there are few babies who are born, eat, sleep, or live by the book. Each baby will have his or her own patterns and idiosyncrasies. As the parent who is creating a baby-centered home it is your job to follow those patterns and let your baby be your guide. A book might tell you that the baby should eat at 11 P.M. and then you should wake him at 3 A.M. and feed him again and he'll sleep until 7 A.M. Well, some babies might do that but other babies might eat all the time and seem to sleep almost never. And your friend or neighbor who had a baby the same day as you may have a baby who has a different pattern from yours. There is no one way. The only problem I see with babies during the first two weeks at home is that I think they should smile and say thank you at 3 A.M! (Unfortunately, they won't be doing any smiling until six or seven weeks.)

As soon as you get home, do a few things. First, put a message on your answering machine that says, "Hi, he was born, his name is Kevin, he's eight pounds, and we're all fine. Leave a message or, remember that casserole you made for Thanksgiving? We'd love to see one on our doorstep." Second, put a handmade sign on your door that reads: "It's a boy! His name is Kevin, he's eight pounds. Leave a casserole on the doorstep."

Another thing to do is put your doctor's number on speed dial. If you have questions, don't hesitate to call your doctor. Call at any hour of the day or night. If you can wait until the morning, call then. But, if you are worried at 3 A.M. call your doctor. It's our job to respond to your worries and your concerns even at three in the morning. Many of your questions will come from something we forgot to tell you. Oops, we forgot to tell you that a three-day-old baby boy might have urine that looks like blood. Oops, we forgot to tell you that your three- or four-day-old daughter might have a bloody vaginal discharge. Oops, we forgot to discuss certain things with you about feeding schedules and nighttime, so call. Call when you need to. Make it your mantra: Call the doctor when you need to. Refer to books if you have them but if you have doubts and worries, call your doctor.

What Mom Needs

Now you are home with your baby. You're letting the answering machine pick up most phone calls and you have probably had a few visitors and people who are offering help. They say, "Can I do anything to help?" The automatic answer is usually, "No, I'm okay, but thanks anyway." Do not answer automatically. Say, "Actually, that delicious casserole you make would be terrific." Or, ask for help with birth announcements, thank-you notes, laundry, or picking up the dry cleaning. Whatever you need—ask. Imagine if your best friend just had her baby and how willing you would be to help out. Some people will be thrilled to do anything for you and this will allow you to stay with your baby—even if you are taking a nap.

The people who have had babies will understand that you need your rest. The last thing you need to do when your baby is taking a nap is to chat or have tea with somebody or to do housework. Your baby might nap for an hour or three hours. If you are busy during that time, when the baby wakes up and needs your attention you will be tired. Get your naps when the baby naps. Basically, during the first two weeks you will be napping and nursing, nursing and napping.

Make sure that everybody who walks in your front door or gets within five feet of your baby washes his hands first. Keep children away from your baby. Do not allow anyone who is coughing or sneezing near your baby. And don't rely on anyone's common sense. People will bring over sneezing kids in November to see your baby. They will be sneezing or coughing and pretend they have an allergy just to see your baby. Make it clear they are not allowed in the house if they are sick. It is hard enough to take care of a cold in a three- or four-year-old, let alone in a three- or four-day-old or three- or four-week-old baby.

That said, you don't have to lock yourself in. Don't buy

into the myth that you need to stay inside for six weeks and your baby shouldn't be outside for the first month or two. You can take walks with your baby. In fact, I recommend that you go outside every day with your baby. You can use a baby carrier or, as long as your baby is lying flat and his head and neck are supported, you can put him in a pram or stroller. Avoid people, avoid crowds, avoid busy restaurants, avoid shopping at Christmastime, but take walks around the block and get fresh air. If it's summertime cover the baby's head with a nice little hat and avoid the noonday sun. If it's winter, dress appropriately. Getting outside will be good for you and good for the baby.

Nursing, Pee, and Poop

Your breast milk starts to come in on day one to four. A lot of extra activity can slow down the milk coming in. A lot of worry can also slow down your milk from coming in. I've seen families who have had visitors from out of town when the baby was born. The visitors wanted to go sight-seeing and so the mother packed the three-day-old baby in the car seat and took them sight-seeing, not giving herself any time to rest and recuperate. The result was that her milk did not come in well.

If you have any problems breast-feeding, you can get help from the following lactation consultant resources:

International Board of Lactation Consultants Examiners. Website: www.iblce.org, e-mail address: iblce@iblce.org, telephone: 703-560-7330;

La Leche League. Website: www.lalecheleague.org, telephone (in this country): 1-800-laleche; (in Canada): 1-800-665-4324; for Canadian French–speaking: 514-laleche.

Your obstetrician can get you a referral to a lactation consultant. Or, ask your pediatrician. Lactation consultants are covered by some insurance.

During the first few days, babies may not pee much but they will poop. The early poop is meconium, which is a thick, tarry poop and the by-product of months of building a baby. It is thick and tenacious, and if it dries on your baby then you will practically have to chisel it off. It is industrial-strength poop. At day three or four the stool goes from being tarry black or dark green to a loose yellow, orange, brown, or green stool, much like mud. Breast-feeding babies never have solid poop and they go frequently—every hour or two or more.

Once Mom's milk is in, babies start to pee and they pee a

lot. A baby can pee seventy or eighty times a day, three or four times an hour. You do not have to change seventy or eighty diapers. You change a diaper when it is wet or every time the baby has pooped because it can be more irritating to the skin. Of course, if your baby is crying then one of the first things you should check for is a wet diaper.

The Two-Week Check-Up

I like it very much if both parents come into the office with their baby for every check-up. I don't think that either the mother or father should get secondhand information. I try to schedule appointments in such a way that will suit both parents, including working parents. Check with your doctor about evening hours or Saturday hours. It is always great if both parents are there for these important visits to the doctor and celebrations of the baby's development.

At the two-week check-up I will listen to the baby's lungs and heart. I will look in her ears, eyes, and mouth and make sure all systems are go. Sometimes what parents are more concerned about isn't the baby but what's happening with them. Some of the two-week check-ups I do are tricky because I've seen parents fight over every single thing that goes on. An example is nighttime parenting. Parents learn very quickly that they are not "off" at night. You are always parents—even at three in the morning. You always have choices when your baby wakes up at 3 A.M. You can get up with a smile or fight all the way. People might think you are crazy to wake with a smile at three in the morning when you have only been asleep for a couple of hours, but it's the good kind of crazy. You can clench your teeth and lose an extra hour of sleep or you can sigh and say, "Ah, my baby." I recommend the latter. Remember there is no schedule during the first two weeks (and possibly during the whole first year). Babies have a new schedule each and every day. Sometimes, a parent will call me and say, "He's eleven days old and he's never done this before." Well, he's only been around ten days, so "never" is relative. You are going to see things on day eleven that he didn't do in his first ten days and things on day twelve that he's never done before either. I encourage parents to try their best to be flexible and as long as the baby is peeing and pooping, then he's okay.

The two-week check-up gives me a great opportunity to talk to the parents about any problems that have occurred and to discuss anticipatory guidelines (the next visit will be at six or eight weeks). I prefer to schedule one or two children each hour for check-ups so that I can spend as much time as possible discussing growth and development, pediatric nutrition, and anticipatory guidelines and safety. I highly recommend that you choose a pediatrician who will schedule as much time as you need to talk about things. Make a list of questions to take with you and be sure your doctor answers all of them before you leave.

At the two-week check-up a lot of babies have regained

their birth weight and some have not. When I see a baby who is a few ounces over her birth weight I have three vital pieces of information:

1. Mom has lots of milk and probably knows it since all of her shirts have little spots on them;

2. She's connecting very nicely with her baby; and

3. The baby looks great because his or her body systems are working well.

At this point the parents and I have a nice discussion about the first couple of weeks—how things are going as well as any questions or issues they might have. The most important thing I do is talk to parents about what is going to happen between now and the next time I see them—to forewarn them that certain things might look wrong but not to worry if the baby wants to eat a lot and not poop much. I don't want them to worry (even though most parents will anyway). I want to alert them to things that might look okay but are cause for concern like a baby who wants to sleep a lot and doesn't want to eat much. Some people might tell you it's great to have a baby like this but it is not great. A baby should be up and talking to you. She should be awake every one, two, or three hours to eat. Even though it might look or feel wrong, it is right for them to be up often. I tell parents to resist the advice of people who will tell them it isn't right.

Development at Two Weeks

Babies are dominated by reflexes and two-week-olds are no exception. They do not have a lot of control over their bodies. In order to get voluntary muscle control, you have to suppress very strong reflexes, whether you are talking about little knee-jerk reflexes that we are all familiar with or the facial muscle reflexes you see in a baby. The cerebral cortex, the highest center of the brain, is responsible for putting a lid on all the lightning bolts that make your baby's hands jitter and his mouth make funny shapes when he is trying to smile at you. The cerebral cortex initially begins to allow for eye movement. If you look at your two-week-old baby's eyes they move differently than they did when he was first born. Your baby can track you a bit better now, and watch as you move through the room, then one eye will go left and the other goes right. It's obvious that at two weeks of age the baby's eye muscles are not well controlled.

Over the next four or five weeks the lower facial muscles will become voluntary, giving the most major milestone of them all—the smile. This is a big deal to moms, dads, siblings, and grandparents. It's a big deal to anyone who has been on the receiving end of one of those early smiles.

The baby's intestinal tract will also begin to change. Breast milk is the perfect food to aid in this development, because as the intestinal tract matures, there is almost no waste since it absorbs and digests everything. Breast milk is custom-made for this purpose. Baby poop is mostly mucus and bile along with little curds from Mom's milk that look like seeds. A fair number of babies will poop only once every three days, which can be a surprise to parents. I've seen plenty of babies who only poop once a week. Don't worry. Your baby will be peeing anywhere from forty to eighty times a day so there will be plenty of diapers to change—poop or not.

By the next time I see the baby at two months of age, she is a different little person. It's easier on the parents because they've gotten the grins and conversation they've expected. Between two and six weeks, the baby's voice will change. At the beginning the baby's best word is a grunt. It gets the point across. The baby gets fed and changed by grunting at you. It will be some time before she coos and gurgles. I have read some books that describe an eleven-month gestation. In other words, the baby is still in somewhat of a fetal stage until two months of age. Some parents are even a little disappointed because they expected to have a more babylike person come home and instead they have a very fetal person. By the two-month check-up the baby is no longer a fetal person.

The Two-Month Check-Up

The next visit in my office is at two months of age. By this time parents have adjusted some. Nobody ever completely adjusts to getting two or three hours of sleep, but the parents usually have accepted it. The dad has probably figured out that it is better to have the baby in their bed because he gets more sleep. Mom has definitely figured out that it is better to have the baby in the bed because she doesn't want to get out of bed, put on her robe and slippers, go into the other room, pick up the baby, and nurse her. The baby may nurse more or less frequently in bed. Some moms can't even tell you for sure whether or not the baby is nursing more or less because all they do is roll over and find the baby a breast and then they go back to sleep. Sometimes Mom has to change the baby at these feedings, sometimes she doesn't.

At the two-month visit I like to discuss growth and development again. Again, I will check his eyes and ears, and listen to his lungs and heart. And I will check his legs. By this time the baby's eyes are stronger. The baby will look you right in the eye. Babies usually don't grin too much at this time. However, the first two months of development are amazing. Babies learn how to smile, eat better, move a little more, and hold up their heads and necks. I show the parents this by balancing the baby on my lap to show how the baby can control his head. I bring the baby back and the baby brings his head forward. The baby can control his head in a lateral plane. I bring the baby over to the left and he can bring it back to the right. This is a subtle, but big, milestone.

If you eat while holding your two-month-old in your arms, he will recognize that you are eating and will try to eat your shirt. A baby knows you are eating. Over the next couple of months, between the two- and four-month visit, the development dwarfs the first two months. The baby starts to see farther, hear better, and begin to integrate sights and sounds. The baby understands that's Mom's voice and the other voice is Dad's. Babies begin to recognize patterns.

At a check-up of two weeks or two months of age, I think I do my best work from five feet away. In fact, I encourage parents to have someone hold their baby and step back a few feet. It's easy to get caught up in a little dot of a rash or whether or not his ears are symmetrical. I'll wager that if you look at your baby from a few feet away, you will be very pleased at what you see.

My job is very joyous because in pediatrics things tend to not go badly wrong. There can be issues, questions, and problems, but the problems are usually not large. During the first two months of a baby's life I will probably see her more times than I will ever see her again. I will see her in the hospital on day one or so; I will see her at two weeks of age; my lactation consultant will probably make a house call after mom and baby are home; and I will see her at two months of age. Basically, these meetings become more like celebrations. Celebrations of the birth; celebrations of the progress parents and baby have made as a family; celebrations of the baby's smiles (at two months); celebrations of the fact that things are beginning to get just a little smoother.

Summary

Everything changes hour by hour, day by day when your baby is two days, two weeks, and two months old. Be very flexible. Listen closely to what your baby needs. Respond to your baby as much as you possibly can. Take the best possible care of yourself in those first two days and two weeks at home. If you want to, you can think of yourself as two separate people. You are in fact yourself, but you are also your baby's mom and everybody needs to take the best possible care of your baby's mom.

CHAPTER SIX

The Classic Four-Month-Old

As the baby approaches four months of age I do another visit. This is my favorite breakthrough visit with your baby. I've told my office staff that if they do nothing else for me on Monday morning, try to schedule a four-month-old visit, because when I walk into the room the four-month-old will grin at me as if to say, "Hi! Good to see you!" The baby grins and smiles at me as if I'm absolutely the prince of his world. However, I have to remember to not take it too personally because a four-month-old baby will also grin and giggle if he sees a stick in the ground, if the cat walks by his nose, or if someone is wearing a hat he takes an interest in.

Four-month-old babies are the sweetest little humans you ever want to see. They are fun. If you are not having fun with a four-month-old, then I think there is probably something wrong with you! They grin, giggle, and look right at you. Their visual and sensory radius has expanded tremendously—from about four feet to twenty feet. While they are interested in everything they can't always find or localize the sound. They hear you, and they hear the dog barking, and they will look for you but they won't turn immediately to see Dad there on the left or Mom on the right. They are so alert and so aware of their surroundings that they are the most fun to take to the park or on a trip.

It's great to travel with a four-month-old because they will charm everyone on the airplane. The other passengers will see a baby on board and say, "Oh, my gosh, there's a baby on board." And be worried that their flight will be a nightmare. But soon a four-month-old will charm everybody. They establish an immediate relationship with anyone they lay eyes on from Grandma to Uncle Bob to the mailman. Everybody loves four-month-olds because they grin and giggle.

The scariest visit that I do at four months of age is a "blah" visit when a baby keeps his hands down and is not interested in much. These babies usually turn out okay but may need to be looked at a little differently by the doctor. If your baby isn't giggling, laughing, and swatting at things, you need to prod your doctor to find out why.

By this age, if there were any worries or anxieties or neurological concerns they dissolve, because at four months of age all systems in a baby are on the surface. It should be very obvious that your baby can see farther and hear better, is integrating sights and sounds, is talking more and speaking in longer sentences of gibberish, and your baby's physical being has changed.

At the four-month visit we talk a lot about sleep. Babies sleep differently at four, five, and six months of age than normal people do. They do not sleep through the night. They like to wake up. They like to talk. They like to eat. They need lots of calories for their development. They love to have contact with people, especially Mom and Dad. And there is nothing wrong with that.

It would be wonderful if we could all wake up in the middle of the night and someone would give us a hug and a snack and ask us if we wanted more. We don't get that as adults, but babies do. And they should. People imply that there is something wrong with this but there isn't. Babies need to eat when they need to eat and sleep when they need to sleep. You need to listen to your baby and find her new four-month schedule. Don't wean or change nighttimes or modify sleep on someone else's schedule. Don't let anyone talk you out of the family bed now that your baby is four months old. I happen to think the family bed is for every-body, unless you are a heavy drinker or like to smoke in bed.

We are the only culture and the only species who kick our young out of bed before they are ready. There is no other culture—European, Asian, or African—that sets up separate sleeping quarters for their babies. There are certainly no other animals who move their young out before they are able to take care of themselves. The idea of it flies in the face of good parenting instincts and in the face of good science. In fact, despite what some doctors or experts will tell you, there is no basis in fact or in science that a baby needs to sleep away from you to learn to soothe himself to sleep, to sleep better, to avoid developing bad sleep habits, or to avoid the danger of sleeping in your bed.

Between the two- and four-month visit the change in a baby is huge. At this age they don't need anything other than breast milk. It will be obvious if your baby is growing nicely and he will probably have gained about a pound a month. And while some babies will double their birth weight by the four-month check-up, others will not. However, on the aver-age a seven-pound baby (at birth) will grow into a twenty-one-pound one-year-old. Again, on average about one pound a month, more or less.

Eye-hand coordination has not developed at four months of age but a four-month-old will often wave her hands around. She may not grab a rattle every time she tries but she will want to. You can see it. If you dangle something in front of your baby sometimes she will grab it and at others she will wave her hands as if to say, "This hand worked yesterday and I wonder why it doesn't work today?" The milestone is the intention to grab rather than the actual grabbing of the rattle. But when they grab the rattle they will love to shake it and they will also learn to transfer the rattle from one hand to the other.

A four-month-old baby is more upright. A lot of babies at four months of age will not be happy unless you stand them up. They have a real interest in prephysical frustration. Your baby knows how to sit, crawl, and walk but for the moment it is locked in her brain and isn't translated to physical activity. The parallel that I draw is to the preverbal twenty-month-old baby who understands all your words, but can't talk. Your four- to six-month-old baby believes that she should be put down on the floor so she can crawl, when actually she can't even roll over. That frustration is obvious on the changing table when the baby does a little one-inch sit-up or swats at things and can't quite get them. It's a time when a baby is really learning a lot about her body but isn't quite happy. In fact, she's pretty frustrated. When she is in your arms she may seem to be saying to you, "Put me down and I'll be okay." She is like a little turtle that has landed on its back but thinks it can go anyway. A four-month-old will tell you this by looking at you, talking to you, swatting at you, and wriggling in your arms. They want to roll. They want to reach out and grab everything. Your baby is becoming more like his parents and everybody around him. He is becoming a vertical person and is beginning to relate to people differently. He is able to sit in your arms and enjoys standing up. Your baby's body is a lot more in his control, because he is able to move it a little bit and is happiest sitting up or standing. They are active and exploding developmentally.

The downside of this is that a baby may learn to roll before you expect him to. Babies roll the day after they couldn't. I phrase it this way because I get phone calls from parents saying they have always left him on the bed with a pillow on either side to keep him from rolling off, but the next thing they know he rolled off the bed and onto the floor. Watch it. Babies who can't roll one minute can roll the next.

By four months of age the baby starts to recognize patterns. The brain just jumps. A baby starts to recognize that when Mom walks into the room she does or says certain things and when Dad walks into the room he does or says something different. When the baby hears the water running and his clothes come off he knows it's bath time and he will wiggle his backside because he usually loves his bath.

With the recognition of patterns the baby also understands that she is the safest human being that ever lived because she gets hugged and cuddled. When usual patterns of behavior break, such as when you put your thumb in your ear and wiggle your hand or do some silly thing, she won't perceive danger and find the break in the pattern funny.

Your baby giggles when you make a funny noise or

movement; when she sees the dog or cat walk in the room she may get hysterically entertained, because babies love watching patterns and they have no fear when the pattern breaks. This is the time for parents and siblings to metaphorically break out all their old jokes and silly songs because you have a brand-new audience in a four-month-old. The four-month-old baby will not only smile at you, he likes to laugh with you. Don't attempt to entertain him with subtle humor or language-based humor. Rather he loves funny little movements, singing, and eye contact. Babies of this age are much more attuned to facial expressions and unexpected movements.

Parents often ask what the best toys are for this stage. I tell them that a wooden spoon is a great toy. Babies are not interested in complicated toys. Four-month-old babies love rattles because they are discovering cause and effect and they like to make things happen. They learn quickly that when they hold the rattle in their hand and move it they will hear a noise. They love to discover that when they bat at a hanging object it will swing. A four-month-old will love to have a safe little place with objects hanging down that he can hit or kick.

Between two and four months of age babies develop much more language. They begin with one- or two-word sentences and progress to long sentences or paragraphs. Now, what they are "saying" aren't real words and don't have much resemblance to the English language but they *are* communicating. A four-month-old will ask you a question and wait for an answer and then ask another question. One of the sweetest moments you can have with your baby is to talk to him as if he is a real person and have him respond.

Safety

Because babies between four and six months of age are ready to start moving, the biggest challenge is childproofing your home. While she may not be crawling, she will learn to scoot a little bit so you will have to look at your house differently. You have to look at all the sharp corners and edges of chairs and tables. You have to look at where the electrical cords are. You have to sweep your hand under the couch every day to see if there is anything there (like a paperclip) that your baby could eat and choke on. You need to get down on your hands and knees and crawl around on the floor while you imagine yourself as an extremely intelligent, curious, mobile person with little common sense. Your baby will be down on the floor moving (and eventually crawling) around and his attitude will be, "If it's small enough to eat, I'll eat it. If it's too big to eat, I'll bump my head on it." So you get down and you look hard because you want to stay ahead of your baby. The safest thing to do is to childproof before you have to.

If you have pets you have other considerations. Dog and cat hair may not be the greatest thing for some people. If there is a family history of allergies you'll want to reconsider your choice of pets. But cat hair is not dangerous to babies. Dogs and cats rarely harm babies. The dog you have in your house is obviously one you trust. However, babies and dogs should never be left alone together because a baby can surprise a dog with strange noises or poke at their ears, eyes, or nose. Some dogs can get very maternal, and some female dogs have been known to attempt to pick up a baby and take it to another place. Cats learn to stay away from babies to keep from having their tails pulled. Pets are great for kids but don't take a chance and leave your baby alone with your pet.

The Gift of the Four-Month-Old

I had a phone call from the parents of a four-month-old whose eighty-year-old great-grandmother had died and they were wondering if it would be okay for them to take the baby out of town to the funeral. It was winter and they were worried about viruses and the propriety of bringing an infant to the funeral. I advised them to go. When they returned they thanked me and told me that having the baby there reminded everyone about the continuation of life. And that there can be joy amidst sadness. Everyone thanked them for bringing the baby because they felt it was what Great-Grandma would have wanted. A giggling four-month-old had been a bright addition to a somber occasion.

A four-month-old is a very notably developed child. They

have sometimes been unkindly labeled as being in the "village idiot" phase because they have the attitude of, "Hi, how are you doing? I love you no matter who you are." And they giggle—a lot. They have an unbridled enthusiasm for life. This is a crucial phase for parents to develop a sense of well-being in their child, an acceptance of the world as a "good" place in which they are welcomed and loved.

CHAPTER SEVEN

Solid Food and Nutrition

A round four months of age babies become very interested in food. Parents always ask me if it is time to start solid foods because their baby is so interested in what they're eating. I tell them that even if they had a little bit of mud on their plate, their baby would still be interested in it and want to eat it. I usually tell them that I don't think solid foods are a good idea at four months of age.

As previously discussed, I recommend that your baby have only breast milk for the first six months. At six months (and this is not crucial) you can start your baby on solid food. The most important thing to know about solid foods is that you don't have to start at six months. You can start at seven or eight months or later. The next most important thing to know about solid foods is to make it fun. Your baby may want to hold the spoon himself. He may smear food in his hair or on his tray. He may get one tablespoon in his mouth or six. He'll eat what he wants. At this age, everything is a finger food and your baby will be curious and want to explore the color, texture, smell, and taste of food. I tell parents to wear an old shirt, put a shower curtain on the floor, and allow their baby to fully experience their food.

I have seen books that make feeding a baby sound like rocket science. It is actually pretty simple. You can get those very convenient organic baby foods in a jar, but I think it is easier to buy your own locally grown organic fruits and vegetables and prepare them yourself. Remember to wash your hands thoroughly and make sure all the surfaces you use to prepare the food are clean. All you do is steam the food longer than you would if you were preparing it for yourself and then mash it. You can use a fork, a food processor, meat grinder, or food mill. You can give your baby one tablespoon of applesauce on Monday, then two on Tuesday, and wait a few days and give him sweet potatoes. You should introduce only one food at a time so you can watch for food allergies. Fruits and vegetables are almost always nonallergenic, so if you feed sweet potatoes and applesauce—gentle, bland solids of fruits and vegetables—to a six- to seven-month-old baby, I don't really believe you need to wait a day or two between applesauce and sweet potatoes. I really don't believe you need to wait a few days between new foods until seven and eight months when you introduce grains. Whereas almost nobody is allergic to sweet potatoes, applesauce, or pureed broth, there are a fair number of people who are allergic to wheat, rice, corn, or barley, and you should wait two or three days between one grain and the next. I also recommend that when you start cereal grains, you add prune juice to every last serving of oatmeal or rice cereal. It's a great habit. More doctors recommend starting with cereal because of a misunderstanding decades ago about iron needs and adding iron to rice cereal with the thought that babies would do better. Actually, cereal is harder to digest, causes more constipation, and is more allergenic. Fruits and vegetables should be the first solids, not cereal.

If you do use prepared foods, I recommend giving your baby single foods, not combination foods (like a baby food that mixes rice and prunes in the same jar). Single foods are better, from the allergy standpoint, and because you are feeding this little person new foods for the very first time. The only thing you may need to add to a single steamed and mashed food is a little bit of breast milk or water to make it smoother, then let him use a spoon or his fingers to eat it.

At eight or nine months of age babies are ready for foods that are a little chunkier, but this will vary for every individual. Some babies need very smooth food between ten and twelve months because they may not be able to handle little chunks of carrots or pieces of cereal yet. There is nothing wrong with feeding a baby very smooth food all through the first year. Some babies are ready for foods with thicker consistencies at eight or ten months and some are not. Watch your baby and see how he reacts.

You can feed your baby three times a day with the family or once a day or ten times a day. It's okay if you forget to give him solid food one day as long as he gets breast milk. Many baby books imply that it is crucial that a baby eat at a certain age or certain month—I disagree. One book will tell you to breast-feed before solid foods and the next will tell you solid foods first followed by breast milk. Either way is fine. Some days your baby will have less breast milk and more fruits and vegetables. Other days it will be the reverse. Remember to listen to your baby and you will find out what your baby wants.

Fruits and Vegetables

I recommend only fruits and vegetables at this age and not rice cereal or other grains because of the difficulty in digesting the proteins in grains that can in turn develop into allergies later on. While grains don't have a lot of protein, they have more than fruits and vegetables and are harder to digest. Fruits and vegetables are easier to digest and it's never too early to start your child's good eating habits. When you do start grains, wait a few months and start them slowly.

Start with foods that are a little bit bland and sweet, like applesauce and sweet potatoes or other mashed fruits and vegetables. Mashed banana is a tradition, but you can also puree some steamed broccoli. It took me thirty years to learn to enjoy Brussels sprouts but maybe your baby can enjoy them the first year. It is fun to realize that between seven and nine months of age your child can experience twenty different fruits and vegetables and will establish some eating habits that are great for the rest of her life.

Foods to Avoid

The fruits and vegetables to avoid are tomatoes, citrus fruits, and strawberries, not only because of the allergy factor but also because of the acidity factor. You may need to go slowly with other berries or make sure they are very mushy because they are very acidic. Peanut butter is an unhealthy food. It's traditional, it's ubiquitous, but unhealthy. Not only is it almost pure fat, but the protein is highly allergenic, and for some people nearly deadly. The fatty acid content of peanut butter is potentially toxic to humans, mildly toxic at the least, and peanuts themselves can grow aflatoxin, a carcinogenic mold, when they are stored. Peanut butter is a bad food. If you eat it, start late in childhood and don't make it a large part of a child's diet. The same thing with peanuts.

I have a bias against dairy in a child's diet. That bias needs to be somewhat soft-peddled in America because dairy products are a universally fed food. At the very least, avoid cheese and whole-fat dairy because that fat is way too much. Dairy protein is allergenic. We know that. The earlier a child gets dairy products, the more likely they are to have some sort of reaction to it. If you believe in using dairy products, start after the first birthday, and if possible use only yogurt and not whole milk. Children do not need whole milk. They do not need that for the developing brain. That myth is old, was never true, and has been discredited.

Wheat is a common allergen. Start late, go slowly, give rice first, give oatmeal next, and give wheat as the last grain and watch your baby closely, especially for changes in the baby's stool. In addition to stool consistency, you should watch for rashes, indigestion, and extra gas.

Human beings should not eat hot dogs. Five- and six-year-olds understand this when we talk about what we grind up and stick in a hot dog. Hot dogs are prototypically the perfect food for choking a child. They fit right into the trachea in some kids. I do not recommend hot dogs in any way, shape, or form for children. If you are using nonfat tofu dogs or other nonmeat hot dogs, start late—after three or four years of age. At nine to ten months of age, when a child is beginning to eat solid foods, which are a little less mushy and a little less liquified, be very careful! A child shouldn't eat grapes. Cut grapes in pieces after the first birthday if you are going to give your child grapes. There is nothing wrong with a child having a very soft diet well through the first twelve months of life.

Cereal

A month or two after starting solid foods buy organic rice cereal or oatmeal and definitely leave wheat for last. I recommend to parents that when they start grains to add prunes or prune juice to their baby's diet or they'll be sorry. There is nothing better for constipating a baby than rice cereal.

Eating for Life

At nine months of age I recommend looking at the family diet and what you will be feeding the baby and get everybody on the same track. A good diet for a nine-month-old would be fruits, vegetables, pasta chopped up very fine, and mashed beans of any kind. You can roll the mashed beans into little balls or smash them into patties. Tofu is very high in protein and low in fat, and although very untraditional in America, it is very good for your baby (and you!). The only seasoning to avoid is salt but all others, like garlic and onion, are good. Olive oil is good in moderation. Babies don't need any oil but if you want to do a little quick sautéing, use a little olive oil.

All through the first year or years of life, you can feed a baby a nearly perfect diet. At a baby's birthday you might want to make a really healthy cake and that's fine. I eat cake on my birthday—it's only once a year.

Summary

Nutrition is the cornerstone of good health. Your doctor should know a lot about nutrition, you should learn as much as you can about your child's nutrition, and then you should relax. The most important thing I tell people about feeding solid foods to a six- to seven-month-old baby is you don't have to. You can start solid foods at six or seven or eight months. You can feed a baby solid foods as often or as little as works for you and the baby. A baby can do very nicely on breast milk alone for the first six to twelve months of life. But, have a good time with solid foods!

CHAPTER EIGHT

The Classic Six-Month-Old

Your six-month-old is a developmental marvel. He has developed new skills, which are classic physical attributes, sensory skills, and mobilizations. Your baby can sit and roll. He can reach out and purposefully grab something, manipulate a toy, grab Dad's hair, poke Mom in the eye or mouth, and annoy Big Brother. They are more interested in toys. They like to bang things around. They like music. They love to listen to you sing and try to imitate you singing.

The sensory skills are now classic. Your baby sees farther and hears better and can localize sights and sounds and put these together. Your baby can turn quickly to the left when he hears his dad's or mom's voice. Often he will look toward the door when he hears the sound of a doorbell. The six-month-old brain has changed so much that some seven-, eight-, or nine-month-old kids will always look up when they hear the sound of an airplane or the sound of a bird. These are classic shifts in sensory skills. There's a gigantic brain change to realize that the sound of an airplane makes him look up and to the left or right.

Between six and nine months of age there is a huge acceleration in fine and gross motor skills. What this means for you is that you need to be even more vigilant about safety in the home. When a baby develops the ability to pick up things with his forefinger and thumb anything left on the floor is potentially dangerous. The rule is that if there is a recently deceased moth on the carpet it will look edible to your baby. So you have to look at your floor completely differently. With the development in gross motor skills you now have a baby (by nine months) who can pull up to standing but who will then promptly fall over. You need to look around the house again so that there are no exposed hard edges on the tables or your fireplace. You will need to learn to put everything out of your baby's reach and you will be telling everyone, "Please put it where she can't reach it."

At six months of age a child is beginning to be aware of language. They understand that there is at least one important word—their name. Your daughter realizes that "Mary" is one really important word. Or it may be the word *boo-boo* if that is one you use a lot. Any word that goes next to the word *Mary* is therefore important. Babies from six to eight months of age are acquiring language. They may learn ten to thirty words so when you say, "Where's Daddy?" she might think, "I know I am Mary so the other person must be Daddy." You might say, "You are going to take a bath, Mary." The baby thinks, "Okay, that's bath over there because I am Mary over here." You can watch your baby learn words. While they don't talk at all they make the effort to watch your mouth closely to see how you do it so they can later replicate the sound. You can say, "bath" or "Mary" or "dog" whenever you want and see the baby closely watching your mouth, listening intently, then trying real hard to imitate you. They will fall short of imitating the sound at this stage but that doesn't mean that they do not understand the words—they do. Some six-month-olds start to use consonant sounds at this age. No matter if they have consonant sounds or not, most six-month-olds are "talking" like crazy.

The most classic shift at this stage, as far as I am concerned, is the cognitive/emotional shift—the differentiation of self from others. Six-month-old babies are very much aware that they are separate from the world. The world, rather than being frightening, is much more interesting. They have more fun outside. For the first five months the whole world is an extension of the baby—there is no differentiation. In the early months, your baby might think,

"There is a piece of me over there and you are me and so is that thing and so is Dad and so is the dog." Babies see the world as an extension of themselves. This helps them feel safe and connected.

Around six months of age there is a very loud *click* in the baby's brain alerting him or her to the fact that there are two places in the world. There is "me" and "not me." Some people incorrectly describe this differentiation of self from others as anxiety producing and are careful when showing a baby a new object or introducing him to a new person because he might be afraid. When you are raising a baby in a baby-centered home filled with lots of cuddles and hugs and fostering a feeling of safety in your baby, at six months your baby will have an explosion of curiosity and discovery. Your baby might think, "It might not be a meal but I will bite it to see what it really is." Or, "I have never seen that toy before but Mom is offering it to me so I will check it out." Babies who have been cuddled and hugged will feel safe and excited at the concept of things being different from themselves and will not get anxious.

At the same time there is some truth to the stranger anxiety and rejection that you hear about. However, most babies will react to someone they have not met who wants to be overly familiar. How would you feel if a total stranger came up to you and pinched your cheek and wanted to kiss you? I don't think you would like it any more than your six-month-old.

Grandparents and other relatives can be the worst offenders here. They leap off the plane eager to see the baby they haven't seen in two months and they are all over her. They say, "Here, let me hold the baby," and the baby cries. What you need to tell them is, "Let's sit down for a minute together so she can look at you and remember who you are. She might not want to be held right now but you can see how great she is. When she is more used to you I am sure she'll want you to hold her." It's your job to listen to your baby, and if she doesn't want to be held by someone she doesn't have to be.

I've also had people tell me that their babies have picked up a vibe and do not like someone the parents don't like. Babies are very intuitive. Sometimes they are bothered by somebody really nice, but very often if a baby does not like someone, there might be a very good reason. There are also people who seem to attract babies. Babies will pick up on the fact that this person is respectful of the baby and the baby's feelings or needs. They won't just grab at a baby, they will speak softly, keep a little distance, and let the baby get used to them. Babies deserve that respect.

Summary

The six-month-old stage is truly the most classic age of them all during the first year of life. The sensory changes, the physical, cognitive, and emotional changes are all classic.

Everything is happening all at once. Babies begin teething. If they have been sleeping for long periods of time, they might start sleeping for shorter periods. It's an amazing time as the newly born baby starts to truly wake up to the external world.

CHAPTER NINE

The Classic One-Year-Old

From nine to twelve months of age kids change dramatically. Roughly between nine and eleven months of age your baby will not only be increasingly vertical, but he is also getting much more mobile. He is making decisions about moving around the house. His decisions are not always the best so this is a very important time to ensure that your childproofing is in place. This is a time when your baby will be able to understand and somewhat differentiate between "yes" and "no." He won't necessarily understand the words but he can grasp the concept. This is the time when you can begin teaching your child that there are certain things in your home that are not safe.

This is the time when you can introduce the idea of "almost" to your baby. You can say—to yourself—"For a long time we told you that you could do anything you wanted, but we forgot to add the word *almost*. You can do *almost* anything you want. You can't crawl over and grab that. We told you that you could get up and eat any time you wanted and now we are going to say that you can get up and eat *almost* any time you want to. We told you that you were in charge of every single thing in the house and now we are going to say *almost* everything. We told you that you are the most important person in the world. You still are but by an amazing coincidence you live in a house with two of the other most important people in the world—your mom and your dad. Once in awhile we are going to make decisions for the family and not just for you. Believe me, in the long-term anything that benefits the family will benefit you."

The baby will begin to understand the meaning of almost if you repeat it over and over again, and the way that you do it is to show the baby that you're there to interact with him, to play with him, but you aren't going to interact with him and play with him if he crawls over to the electrical socket or the stereo knob or some other dangerous or inconvenient object. Instead of interacting with him and talking with him, you are going to pick him up and walk away. And you are going to repeat that as many dozens or hundreds of times as you need to in order to reinforce the idea that he gets attention and fun and interaction with Mom or Dad for almost everything in the house, and there are other things that just get him nothing. Babies do not understand the word, but they very slowly begin to understand the idea of almost everything.

The word *almost* applies to the nine-, ten-, eleven-, or twelve-month-old baby even though they don't understand it.

The One-Year Check-Up

The one-year check-up is another really big deal. At one year your child may be walking and it is a time of great celebration. Yes, it's a little more dangerous when they can walk, but it's something to celebrate nevertheless. At this age kids are crazily exploring the world, their senses are 100 percent alive, and their motor skills have accelerated even more. The pincer grasp of the nine-month-old has expanded into very good toy manipulation. They enjoy all sorts of toys but can't deal with small parts so they like big ones like balls, trucks, and things they can move or push around.

The first birthday opens a little window into the next couple of years of your baby's life. I get more calls at one year of age than at any other transition about behavior problems. Largely this is because parents are realizing that they have another "voter" in the house. The behavior that parents see at twelve months is often how people expect two-year-olds to behave, i.e., being very assertive, very strong-willed, very positive, and not particularly caring about the needs and desires of others. A one-year-old has tremendous strength of will and not a lot of power to reason with us.

For example, if you say to a three-year-old, "Wait a minute, let me finish this and then we will do that," a three-year-old will understand "wait a minute," which is really delayed gratification. By three to three and a half, your independent, self-confident child has a sense of patience and fairness. Your one-year-old has independence and self-confidence but these attributes are not balanced by patience or fairness. He wants what he wants when he wants it. Again, this is behavior that people expect from a two-year-old. However the very best one-year-olds are assertive, strong-willed, huge, powerful little personalities. It is a beautiful thing to step back and say, "Look at this personality! Look at what we've helped to create and nurture over the last twelve months." Unfortunately, if you happen to be trapped in an airplane for three hours with this gigantic personality, sometimes it's not so much fun and even a long car ride or a long afternoon with a gigantic personality can be a real challenge.

What you can do when confronted with this "gigantic personality" is to increase interaction with things that work, that make the family run better in things that you want to encourage, and you don't interact at all when the baby does things that you really don't like. An example of this is that a lot of times what happens is you leave something on the table and your one-year-old sees it and points to it. When your baby points at something and you don't want the baby to have it, don't respond when the baby throws a little tantrum. Don't respond when the baby starts to yell at you. Sometimes you make a mistake and you realize you really didn't need to keep that baby away from what was there; however, the way you help a baby learn is just by being consistent.

Some parents worry that they need to send their one-year-old to a class to improve their socialization skills or to teach them to eat in a socialized way. They don't need it. They don't need to be scheduled. A three-year-old needs schedules. She needs to be in bed at a certain time so she can get up in the morning for preschool and so she doesn't fall asleep at story time. A one-year-old can still be a free spirit. They can eat eight times a day instead of three, they can play at odd hours, they can sleep at odd hours and may want to get up to eat or chat. This behavior may frustrate parents but they can't change it.

Even though your one-year-old may not want to play with a bunch of one-year-old babies—because they will tend to hit each other and take each other's toys—he will love to go to the park and watch other children play. He will like to watch other children's faces. He will love to see big kids playing and running and jumping in the park. Being outside is great for kids of this age as there are so many new sights, sounds, and smells for them to be exposed to. Their brains are moving fast at this age and they are great learners so they like reading with you and they like simple toys. They don't need any toys that are complicated and will frustrate them.

A one-year-old's sleep patterns can change but they don't change much. Again, there is much written about the way they *should* change but they really don't change. In my practice it is much more normal, much more average, for a one-year-old to *not* sleep through the night than for a one-year-old to sleep through the night. One-year-olds have tremendous brain growth, high activity levels, and incredible changes in their daily activities, so they don't sleep well. They probably have bigger dreams. They wake up and want to do things. It's not necessarily good for a one-year-old to sleep through the night even though this might seem like the Holy Grail to some people.

Another issue that generates many phone calls at age one is the complexity of the little human being. The physical complexity is obvious in that learning how to walk is no longer good enough at age one as now she wants to run, climb, and jump—sometimes all at once. Parallel to the physical complexity is an emotional complexity that is amazing. Nine-month-olds have an elegant emotional simplicity. If they are angry or sad, you can flip them. You can make a silly sound or sing a silly song, and they will smile. If you try to make the same goofy sounds for an angry twelve- or fifteen-month-old, they will probably bite you on the hand and move away as if to say, "I'm angry. I've forgotten why I'm angry but I'm really angry." This type of behavior can be perplexing to parents especially when they are used to being able to jolly their child out of a bad mood.

Because the world has gotten so big and because they are now months into the differentiation of self from the mother, some of their fears can arise. They may be bothered by louder noises. They may be bothered by people who move or act very differently. They might even be bothered by dogs and cats. Respect these fears. Go slowly. If your child does not like loud noises make sure people know that. If your child does not like balloons or dogs, avoid them. Read books about balloons or dogs to your child but do not try to introduce or force your child into overcoming fears until the second year of life. The best way to deal with a child's fears is to avoid, if at all possible, situations that scare him. You can't reason with kids during the first two or three years of life; they just don't understand abstract notions that they don't need to be afraid of something or that Mom or Dad will keep them safe from it. So instead, try just to avoid that situation.

Teething is a big-time issue at one year of age because the one-year molars come in. There are two on the bottom and two on the top, which seem to hurt for a longer period of time than other teeth. In all there are twenty teeth that have to come in. If you look in your one-year-old's mouth and you see six to eight teeth, know that there are another twelve to come. Each one of those teeth could hurt a little bit, disrupt sleep, or disrupt mood, so offer your baby as much relief as possible (a frozen washcloth, homeopathic teething tablets, or even baby Tylenol if necessary). This is the age to begin dental hygiene. You can wrap a very thick washcloth around your finger (or you will get bitten) and rub the baby's teeth for about seven or eight seconds. Get the front surfaces and the back surfaces and the molars. This breaks up plaque and decreases the number of cavities your baby could have. Brushing teeth should be fun. Forcing your child to brush her teeth leads to a bad relationship with the toothbrush. Make it fun. Give your one-year-old a toothbrush and say, "I'll brush your teeth and you brush mine."

One-year-old children also have newfound abilities with language. They will speak a few words but understand many more. You have someone in your house who can understand almost everything you say, but can't communicate it to you. However, there are limitations to their understanding. If your one-year-old child hears you say at nine in the morning that you are going to the park in the afternoon, all she will hear is "park," and will expect to be going to the park immediately. She understands the word, but can't understand the context and doesn't have a concept of "later" or "tomorrow" or "this afternoon." A one-year-old will listen closely to all the words but they can't communicate so they can get very frustrated. In fact, tantrums usually come from this preverbal problem. Your child might be saying to you, "I've asked you nicely twice if we could leave the restaurant now, but because you didn't understand me I'll get us thrown out of here." If you listen to your one-year-old, he might grunt and point at something and you can usually understand what he wants. But if you get it wrong the third time, he will make the decision that you are too foolish to talk to and throw himself on the floor in frustration.

The one-year transition brings a lot of feeding changes as well. Babies will have some social eating in that they may have three meals with the rest of the family. They may enjoy restaurants, not necessarily because they like the food but because they enjoy the social setting and it is entertaining. They love to watch other people and they love to watch other kids.

One-year-olds may not eat as much. A common phone call I get about one-year-olds goes something like this: "My one-year-old stopped feeding two days ago." My question is, "What is he doing?" The answer usually is, "He's in the living room, running circles around his daddy." I think to myself, "No problem," and tell the mother that I'm not worried about this kid even if he hasn't been eating because he is running circles around his daddy.

The reason a child stops eating is that his requirement for calories has dropped. Most kids in the first year of life will double or triple their weight. Your twenty-one-pound one-year-old will probably turn into a forty-pound four-year-old so not only will he not double his weight from one to two he won't double it for the next three years. The caloric requirement plummets around the age of one. A child who is dragging himself on the ground and crawling around requires more calories than a child who is walking because the movements are more sophisticated and they need fewer calories to move and fewer calories to grow. A lot of one-year-olds seem to stop eating.

At the age of one year a child can be eating a lot of the foods the rest of the family is eating—fruits and vegetables, grains and beans all mushed up, smashed into patties or rolled into a ball, cut-up pasta, and tofu. A lot of families eat fish and chicken, but I don't recommend red meat at this age, since it's too big a protein and it's not a very healthy protein at all. This isn't entirely magical, but one year of age is the age when babies can have citrus fruits, tomatoes, and strawberries—foods which I like to avoid during the first year of life. Foods get a little less mushy, a little more solid, and babies can handle it.

Juice is not good for babies. It has a lot of sugar. Water is much, much better. Breast milk can be the sole source of liquids but there is nothing wrong with drinking water from a cup or from a bottle. If you would like to, you can completely skip the bottle stage and just give your baby a sip of water. Juice is hard to avoid, but minimize it in your baby's diet.

If a schedule is changing for Mom or Baby, whether it's twelve months of age or earlier, the baby may need to learn how to drink from a bottle earlier. I don't think that you have to insist the baby learn to drink from a bottle. You can use a cup any time after the first few weeks of age, although most people use a bottle if the baby is going to be separated from the mother for work reasons. Before five or six months of age, or even twelve months of age, most people are using a bottle with their babies. It is not crucial to get a baby to be off the bottle in the second year. It might be slightly better for the teeth, but it might not be as damaging for the teeth as we used to say it was. Obviously sucking a bottle of juice all day or all night is not good for the baby or for the teeth, but a bottle of breast milk or a bottle of water will not hurt the teeth.

My best recommendation is to offer good food and pretend you don't care if he eats it. The more energy you invest in trying to get a kid to eat the more likely they are to resist. Simply offer the broccoli, let him know that if he doesn't eat it, you will, and that he doesn't need to finish any food on his plate. There is no specific order that has to be followed in getting a child to eat at age one. A baby doesn't have to know all about eating dinner first and then dessert. A baby can eat foods three times a day or five times a day. There doesn't have to be a specific schedule for eating and a baby doesn't have to learn about eating certain quantities. What is much more important is offering very healthy foods and avoiding unhealthy foods.

At one year of age a father's role broadens. Babies at one year of age are eating a lot of other foods and do not need to breast-feed with every meal. Babies will separate from their mothers and go out and take a walk with Dad. This is a great time to invest in a running stroller or a good backpack and take long Daddy-Baby hikes. It is a great time to continue dad's role as the bather and perhaps the nighttime or part-time caretaker. It is a great time for dads to get more and more involved and it can take a lot of time and energy. It's a great time for dads to get to know their babies better and for doing more with them. However, this doesn't mean taking the easy way out and going for junk food or for dessert.

Summary

The one-year-old stage is the time when you can talk to your baby more about the family and a little bit less about being a dictator. Babies love to be in charge of everything, and this is what I call the "almost" age.

CHAPTER TEN

Socialization, Learning, and Discipline

As I mentioned previously, kids don't need to be "socialized" in the first year or two. Many parents like to go to gymnastics class with their kids or "Mommy and Me" and "Daddy and Me" classes. They are a lot of fun but you might notice it is the parents who tend to have more fun at the classes than the kids do. Kids don't play that well together during the first year or so. They like to watch older children at the park or on the playground, and five-year-olds love to play with one-year-olds, but one- and two-year-olds don't play all that well together. It can be fun to go to classes with your child as she can form some friendships and learn a little about socialization but don't worry if you don't take her to a class. At this age all your child needs is you, not another group of children.

Working moms is a very tricky issue. Current child-rearing thought says we should spend as much time as we can with our baby. Six weeks' maternity leave is ridiculous, impractical, immoral, not good for babies, and not good for moms. Moms who have to go back to work when a baby is two or four or ten months of age are going to have to make some compromises about feeding, and day care and baby-sitting and cups and bottles and breast-feeding. You just have to do the very best you can! A baby will learn how to accept a bottle from somebody else. Probably the ideal time is between the age of four to eight weeks of age if you know you are going to have to go back at eight weeks of age or earlier than that. It's difficult to get a baby to accept a bottle at four or six or ten months of age if they have never had one. Those babies will take to a cup. The babies will not starve themselves or dehydrate themselves. If they want to hold out, they can hold out and then they will come to you. Some babies will wait if they know Mom is coming home and they want to breast-feed. It's okay—they will not hurt themselves. Find the best day care or the best baby-sitter, or the best nanny care you can find. Find someone who is very interested in interacting with your baby. If it is a day-care setting, get the best possible ratio of caretakers to babies that you can. Babies require a great deal of time and energy and someone who has to take care of six to eight babies is not going to be able to give your baby the attention that he or she needs. You're going to have to make some compromises. My strong encouragement is to find a situation where you can get back to work as late as possible and as much part-time as possible. This is not practical advice and it is not even compassionate advice for some people. But do the very best you can.

The brain in the first year or two of life is astonishing. Children can learn two or three languages more easily than we can pick up one. If you speak a second language make sure your child is exposed to it as much as possible, or if you know someone—such as a baby-sitter, friend, or relative who speaks Spanish or French—ask them to only speak that language around your child. At age two or three he might get confused and mix English words with words from the foreign language, but the long-term benefits are huge.

In the first two years of life the brain will accept huge amounts of information when offered by a parent or anyone who is gentle and kind to the child. Children love to hear about things and to listen to your voice. Reading to a child is crucial throughout the first years because it is a wonderful habit to develop—for both you and your child. Also, books allow you to spend time with your child discussing information, people, places, and things that you might not otherwise encounter. Reading to a child presents an opportunity for them to learn more than we might expect.

Around six to nine months of age children know about object permanence, meaning that an object exists outside of their plane of vision. This concept enables her to play "peek-a-boo" with an object without frustration, which means you can put an object behind your back and then bring it out and she will laugh. She will never tire of playing this. At this age they also enjoy riddle and hand-clapping games, singing, movement, and gentle bouncing. Noise, but not too much noise, is also enjoyable.

Because a nine- or ten-month-old loves to see different places you can take them to the grocery store or gas station or park because they look, smell, and sound different from home. Talk to your child when you are out and about and point out trees, and dogs, and cars and people. Let him touch the leaves and feel the grass. You don't need special or expensive toys at this age because he will gain so much from going places, seeing new things, and sharing that time with you talking about the things you are seeing together.

Around nine to ten months of age children develop another very interesting milestone, the voluntary release from the hand. If you fill up both of a six-month-old child's hands and offer him a third object that might be more attractive to him, he will either reach for it with his mouth or get very angry because his hands are full. He has not yet developed the ability to drop one item and reach for the next. A nine-month-old will drop items at will. The downside of this milestone is that it will rapidly contribute to his ability to play the classic game of, "I'll drop this and you (Mom) will pick it up." This is a game he will want to play for hours and you will tire of it long before he does.

The reason this little drop-and-fetch game holds his attention for so long is because to him, gravity is being invented every time he drops something. A child learns that it doesn't matter if it is sweet potatoes or a toy, when you drop it you can pick it up again because it is right next to your hand. But when he drops (or throws) something from the high chair it ends up four or five feet away. This is fascinating for him and he will never tire of dropping and throwing games.

He will also not understand the reality of gravity as it applies to himself. He won't quite understand why, if he's not careful when he walks, he will fall down and hit his nose. One-year-olds won't walk around things but will walk into things—including walls—because they don't understand the concept of danger. Their sense of self-preservation is not highly developed so as his parents you need to step in and steer him from danger. As an aside about walking I'd like to add that shoes are not necessary for a one-year-old who is taking those first tentative steps. Walking barefoot is best because he will learn to balance and strengthen the muscles and tendons of his feet and ankles. If any footwear is needed then you can put leather-bottomed socks or soft moccasins that will prevent him from slipping but promote development.

At nine months of age you will see the beginnings of the

limit-testing phases. Your child will become a limit tester and it is your job as a parent to become a limit setter. Unfortunately, this is also a time when parents make mistakes. What will usually happen is that the child will crawl twenty times over to an electrical socket, stereo knob, or other forbidden object and the parent will say "no" twenty times. On the twenty-first time the typical parent will get angry and yell "no," shake their finger at the child, give him a lecture, and possibly (although I think it should be illegal) slap his hand. The lesson the nine- or ten-month-old learns from this is, "Gee, what a busy day Daddy is having, but if I go and try to grab this I will get his attention for a few minutes." Then you are in trouble because for the rest of his childhood he has learned the best way to get your attention is to do something you don't like.

Instead, it is best to flip the scenario around and say, "Listen, we give you all the attention and energy you want. We read books to you and we play with toys. Except for those things over there—the electrical socket, the stereo knobs, and a couple of other things—when you crawl over there we say a couple of words like, 'stop it, please' and if you don't we pick you up and move you five or ten feet away and then walk away." Eventually, the child crawls back to the forbidden object. This is the most tedious aspect of parenting because it is not twenty repetitions and you are finished. It is more like 920 repetitions. But if you don't accept this responsibility and set limits 920 times you will end up with a child who doesn't understand limits. This is the age when a child is first able to comprehend the idea or concept of "no." However, if you yell "no" at a child she might laugh because she likes your voice. She may prefer your quiet sweet voice but it is still your voice if you are yelling or not so you can't be lazy about it. You have to get up, pick her up, move her, and do it again and again and again. This is a slow and steady form of discipline that is a little like mini time-outs but it works.

Remember, the behavior you see in a three-year-old may well be the behavior you see in a twenty-three-year-old. And it won't be her fault. She was born a very nice little girl and her parents sat back and said, "If she wants to touch those things we'll just let her touch them." This child will end up hurting herself and probably bother other children as well. She certainly won't be invited to anyone else's house if she can't behave.

The obligation of the parent at eight, nine, or ten months of age is to explain to a child that he or she will actually get more freedom if he or she learns limits. Children will grasp this concept very slowly so you need to reinforce it consistently. You need to say to your child, "We know you want to touch that, but if you go back to the electrical socket we're going to say 'stop it' and we are going to move you again and again until you understand not to go there." You can also prepare a three- or three-and-a-half-year-old for the park by teaching them to understand that the primary park rule is to come when Mom or Dad or the caregiver says, "Come here, please." If he plays that three-year-old game of run when he's called, his freedom in the park will be limited to the length he can run. The only fair thing to do is to start at nine or ten months of age with saying no and repeatedly correcting the child. Because a child learns this concept of limits and freedom slowly, it is important to start young when teaching it.

Corporal punishment—slapping a wrist or spanking—teaches your child that it is okay to hit people. It is never okay to hit people. Trying to explain to a child that it is okay for the parent to hit him because he hit his little sister is very confusing for a child and basically ends up teaching him that it is okay for him to hit people smaller than he is.

Demoting the Dictator

Around nine or ten months of age I talk to parents about demoting the dictator. Until about nine months of age the baby is in charge of everything. If there is a vote it tends to be one against two with the single vote winning the contest. If anyone wants to get up and nurse all night there will be two votes against, but the vote will go in favor of the baby who wants to nurse. In any conflict the baby will win. At this age the baby is very sure he's the most important person in the world and loves voting one to two in favor of himself instead of voting two to one in favor of his own family. I like the idea of making a transition from a 100 percent baby-centered home to about a 90 percent baby-centered home. The baby at this point is a very, very powerful person and he understands that he's a very powerful person and can withstand the concept of "not now—almost."

Around nine or ten months of age you can start having the majority rule where two votes really will decide the outcome. While the baby will probably object to no longer ruling the roost it is the parents' job to strike a balance in the family and have the baby become less of a dictator and more of a democratic contributor.

I don't like putting babies to bed and letting them cry. I like putting them to sleep very gently. I like the family bed for nine to ten months or for two to three years or for however long it works for a particular family. For some people the first birthday is a good transition point and they make the move from the family bed to a crib. At that point I don't recommend a separate room or a closed door. I recommend rubbing and patting and being with the baby rather than closing the door and using a monitor. If a baby goes to bed before the parents and the baby is willing to sleep in the crib or go to sleep in the crib easily without a lot of crying, that might work. If not, a baby can go to sleep with you. I think one of the biggest misconceptions in American child rearing is that there should be some sharp demarcation and separation between parents' time and baby's time or family time. This should be a gentle transition and for at least the first year or two, there's going to be a lot of time when the baby comes first, and this is kind of difficult because there is not a lot of support in America and in the cultural context for this.

Summary

Very slowly, between age one and age three, a baby needs to learn a little bit more about being a social person. They need to learn a little bit more about limits and about interacting with other people.

CHAPTER ELEVEN

Vaccinations and Illnesses

Beginning at birth, most babies in America get vaccinated. The hepatitis B vaccine is given in some hospitals within the first twenty-four hours of life to protect babies against this terrible disease. Most hospitals are now screening the mother to see if she carries hepatitis B antibodies and will then only vaccinate babies whose mothers are hepatitis-B positive. The other babies are left alone and not vaccinated until the two-month doctor's visit.

Vaccinations

Two months is the most common time in America to give babies five separate vaccinations—DPT, IPV, HIB, Prevnar, and hepatitis B.

DPT

DPT stands for diphtheria, pertussis, and tetanus. Diphtheria is a very rare disease that is common in Asia and Africa but that occurs, on average, only once a year in America. The diphtheria part of the vaccine is known as an adjunct in that it helps the immune system respond to the rest of the vaccines. Pertussis is more commonly known as whooping cough. Whooping cough occurred in epidemics decades ago and was occasionally fatal. Today, whooping cough is less common but that does not mean it has been eliminated. Whooping cough causes severe coughing in children anywhere from six weeks to four months of age. It can be a very dangerous illness for babies under six weeks of age and sometimes babies over six weeks of age can end up in the hospital. The current vaccine—the acellular pertussis vaccine—is extremely effective and protects at a rate of approximately 90 percent. Tetanus is also called *lockjaw*, which is caused by a bacterium called *Clostridium tetani*. The classic cause of tetanus is due to stepping on a dirty nail, because the tetanus bacterium cannot live in oxygen. Bacterium are very tiny so that a piece of dirt, even a grain of sand, could harbor bacteria within it. The nail causes a puncture, and the puncture wound plants that piece of dirt or those bacteria in the body. The wound closes over the bacterium under the skin, and the oxygen in the environment will support the growth of tetanus. We don't have many cases of tetanus in America anymore. We are down to a couple of thousand cases of tetanus each year or so and they tend to occur in older people. The danger to your child is very small.

IPV

The next vaccine your child gets is IPV, which is the polio vaccine. Until the 1990s there were two versions of the polio vaccine—the oral vaccine (OPV), which was a so-called "live" virus vaccine, and the IPV, which is an injected and inactivated polio vaccine. The oral polio vaccine was taken off the market because it was the only source of polio in America. A child would get the OPV and the person changing his diapers would contract the disease. While polio remains in some small villages in Africa and Asia, there have been no outbreaks of polio in America since 1979. At the present time there is no polio in the Western Hemisphere and polio is within a few years of worldwide eradication, according to the World Health Organization.

HIB

HIB is Haemophilus influenza B or the so-called *anti-meningitis vaccination*. HIB used to be the most common cause of meningitis in pediatric medicine. HIB can also cause epiglotitis, a severe life-threatening swelling of the throat. When I first started my practice I would see a case of HIB meningitis almost every winter but now it is almost completely eradicated and there has been a drop of over 90 percent of cases of HIB meningitis since the vaccine started.

Prevnar

Prevnar is a relatively new vaccine that is aimed at the pneumococcal bacteria that causes a fair number of ear infections and meningitis. It is a vaccine that has been around for a while but was recommended as a universal vaccination as of the year 2000.

Hepatitis B

There are quite a few types of hepatitis. Hepatitis A is the so-called "food-handler's hepatitis." It's the kind you get from eating the wrong kind of food and can be transmitted by a cook in a restaurant who doesn't wash his hands well. Hepatitis A is not a terribly dangerous disease. Hepatitis B is a very dangerous disease and can cause permanent liver damage and possible liver cancer as a result of having the disease. Hepatitis B is transmitted through high-risk behavior such as unprotected sex and intravenous drug use. Some people have contracted hepatitis B through blood transfusions but this doesn't happen now due to current blood-screening practices.

Your Two-Month-Old and Vaccines

My personal feeling is that your two-month-old baby's immune system is not yet ready to receive these shots and you should wait. I don't like vaccinating babies less than six months of age. This point of view is held by a very small minority of doctors and I recommend discussing vaccines and the timing of when your child will get them with your pediatrician. I don't think it is a bad idea to give the vaccines at a slightly slower pace so as not to overload a two-month-old's system with five shots with seven different components.

New Vaccines and Vaccine Controversy

As of the year 2002 we will probably have a new antidiarrheal vaccine. The rotavirus vaccine was introduced some years ago to prevent one of the more common causes of severe diarrhea. The vaccine, unfortunately, also caused some cases of intestinal obstruction and was pulled from the market. The new rotavirus vaccine will probably be an oral rather than injected vaccination. When the first rotavirus vaccine was introduced, researchers overlooked the fact that breast milk itself contains antirotavirus activity. Breast milk kills rotavirus and prevents the disease better than any vaccine so I feel the vaccine is clearly not needed in breast-feeding babies. The question is whether it is needed in American babies at all.

It is my personal feeling that we have too many vaccines that we are giving too quickly and at too early an age. Most pediatricians and most experts on vaccinations disagree with me. Discuss vaccines at length with your doctor. However, be aware that the subject of vaccines has become a polarized issue and is difficult to discuss. I believe that for the most part, few people, including doctors, are telling you the truth. On the one hand, doctors imply that vaccines are 100 percent effective and 100 percent safe. They aren't. Opponents of vaccines will say that vaccines don't work and diseases like measles, polio, and tetanus in America were on the way out anyway. This is not true. The reason that we don't have these diseases is because vaccines work very effectively.

The problem is that vaccines may have side effects. There are the conventionally accepted side effects that occur one in one thousand or one in a quarter of a million. These accepted side effects of vaccines involve some percentage of babies getting fevers. Some babies get a lump in the leg at the site of the injection. Other babies feel out of sorts and have some symptoms of the disease against which they were vaccinated. There are babies who get a chicken pox vaccine and develop a mild case of chicken pox. Other babies get little fevers and can feel kind of influenzal.

Unconventional side effects can occur because by giving vaccines, you are tinkering with the immune system. The immune system is very sophisticated and we don't know nearly as much about it as we will next year, the year after, or ten years from now. In the meantime, we are not 100 percent sure we are not doing more harm than good when we give lots of vaccines. Certainly, in the 1950s and 1960s the polio vaccine was a godsend and saved hundreds and thousands of lives, prevented millions of cases of polio, and was well worth whatever risks were involved. The same thing can be said of the measles vaccine in the fifties and sixties to seventies. The same can be said of the rubella vaccine which has virtually eliminated fetal rubella syndrome. The same thing can be said of the diphtheria vaccine, even the HIB vaccine. HIB was well worth the trouble despite any side effects because it almost eliminated the number-one cause of meningitis in the first year or two of life. But now we can step back and we can give these vaccines slower and perhaps give fewer of them in the first year of life. The measles, mumps, and rubella (MMR) vaccine has been connected by reputable researchers to an increased incidence of autism. This is a highly disputed and controversial connection, and while we may not yet know the exact correlation, there is most certainly some connection. Parents, therefore, should think hard about their choice and research the latest findings before making a decision.

The unconventional side effects are the ones that I think should be discussed more openly because I think a baby's immune system is not ready for all these vaccines at two months of age. I do not oppose routine childhood vaccinations; I would like us to reconsider the schedule of those vaccines and consider not adding vaccines so rapidly or more than one at a time on the conventional schedule.

DPT, HIB, IPV, Prevnar, and hepatitis B are usually given at the two-month, four-month, and six-month check-ups. At the six-month check-up most doctors no longer give a third polio vaccine but instead wait until the one-and-a-half-year-old visit to give it.

Measles, Mumps, and Rubella

MMR is not usually given until twelve months of age. This vaccine has become very controversial since the recent research is reported to show a link between MMR and autism and arthritis. Again, there are outspoken people on either side of this controversy. On the one hand, opponents of MMR claim that it causes autism and arthritis. While there may be some link, MMR does not cause all forms of autism and arthritis. Those in favor of MMR will say there is no connection between MMR and autism and arthritis. But this isn't true. The truth is there is a disputed, controversial, unproven, and partially refuted connection, and there is definitely research showing some connection between the MMR vaccine and autism.

Hepatitis A and Chicken Pox

The hepatitis A and chicken pox vaccines are also given around one year of age. The hepatitis A vaccine is recommended for people who are involved in exotic travel. Hepatitis A can certainly ruin your vacation but it is not a dangerous disease for children. I don't recommend the hepatitis A vaccination for children but if the parents want it, I will administer it.

The chicken pox vaccine has been around since the early 1970s but it is still considered a new vaccine. It was developed to prevent the disease in children who were receiving chemotherapy for leukemia or were on high doses of steroids because of asthma or cancer. This vaccine was a lifesaver for these children since they could have died from chicken pox—unlike a healthy child.

For many years pediatricians, including the American Academy of Pediatrics, disputed the need for the chicken pox vaccine. We fought against it very successfully but in the mid-1990s that resistance was overcome and the chicken pox vaccine is now recommended—if not mandated—in some states for children.

The problem that we see with chicken pox is that when it was a common childhood illness, a child would get chicken pox; her immune system would respond; her brother, cousins, and classmates would also get it; and her immune system's antibodies (protection against chicken pox) reached such a high level that she would have lifelong immunity. Now we give one shot that we know lasts for twenty to twenty-five years but we don't know if it lasts for thirty to thirty-five years. The fear among pediatricians is that in twenty-five to thirty-five years there will be a very dangerous outbreak of adult chicken pox. Unfortunately, because the disease is practically eradicated now, you might need to get your child the vaccine, but even though he might not contract the disease normally as a child, he may get the disease later as an adult.

The issue of vaccinations was never controversial when I was in medical school or during my residency. In recent years we have recognized that vaccines have more side effects than we first thought. For that reason, there has been a growing group of parents and doctors who would like to rethink vaccination policies in America. Many times the discussion covers global versus domestic use of vaccines. From a global point of view vaccines do much more good than harm. If we were to discontinue polio vaccines in Africa or Asia we would have huge outbreaks of the disease. If we were to stop giving the whooping cough vaccine I believe we would see a return of the disease.

Beyond the global issues I recommend that parents delay

the vaccinations a little bit longer than the recommended schedule mandates and that they consider each vaccine carefully and pick and choose which ones they want their child to receive. I recommend they read as much as possible on both sides of the issue. I recommend the same for you so that you can have a very candid and open discussion with your doctor.

There are a lot of books and a lot of websites on the subject of vaccines. Most books, articles, and websites produce a polarized view of the subject. They tell you that the vaccines are absolutely 100 percent safe and effective, and the other side tells you equally inaccurate statements about how ineffective and dangerous the vaccines are. There are people telling untruths on both sides of the issue. There are people who tell you that the vaccines don't even work. Of course the vaccines work! They work great and that's the reason we don't have measles in America; that's the reason we eliminated polio in the Western Hemisphere. But now we can step back and think harder about it. What I recommend very strongly is that the parents keep an open mind about vaccinations and that they have extensive discussions with their pediatricians about vaccinations.

Routine Illnesses

Babies who are born in the springtime are exposed to a lot of pollen and tend not to catch a lot of colds. The immune system can be desensitized—that's the basis for allergy shots. You give very small amounts of essence of pollen, very diluted pollen subcutaneously, and then the child develops immunity. After the first year or two of life there is some really interesting evidence about local honey. Honey derived from local beehives may help to desensitize because it contains small amounts of pollen which get into the intestinal tract and may make the child less allergic. It is a home remedy that looks like it has some very solid scientific basis.

First babies are not exposed to siblings but second babies get a lot of big-kid illnesses right away. Babies born in October through January are immediately exposed to a barrage of winter viruses. Babies born at this time need breast-feeding even more (if that is possible) because these babies need the mom's mature immune system working for them.

Colds and coughs are innocent and harmless but they can have a tremendous impact on your life. A baby with a cold will eat with greater difficulty, may sleep less, will cough and sneeze, and can be cranky. I recommend that a baby with a cold nurse more often and can benefit from a few drops of breast milk in his nose. A baby with a cold may feel better when he is upright. He may only sleep when you are holding him up, or in the car seat or when you walk with him. I recommend that you breast-feed your baby and keep him cool, upright, well hydrated, and out of the house. Breast-feeding is enough to support hydration even in extreme climates.

There were studies done in Africa with temperatures ranging well over 105 degrees for days and days. The mothers needed to drink lots of water, but the babies could stay very well hydrated on just the breast milk. The cool, moist outdoor air is almost always better for a baby than dry, indoor air. You can also use a humidifier indoors to keep the air cool and moist. Antibiotics are virtually never necessary for a cold or cough. Breast-feeding babies almost never get ear infections and if they do, antibiotics should not be the first line of therapy. In fact, antibiotics obviously are not needed for any viral infection. Most infections babies get are viral infections—common colds, coughs, and intestinal bugs. The first line of defense is breast milk during the breast-feeding period. The next line of defense is herbal or alternative remedies, staying well hydrated, and getting cool, moist air, and sometimes the very best thing I can do as a pediatrician is to do nothing. I examine the baby very closely, observing the way the baby behaves, asking the parents a lot of questions and then stepping back and making sure in my own mind that the baby does not have any serious or significant illness. Then I convince the parents of this fact, give them guidelines as to when they should be more concerned, what they should watch for, when they should call me, and then do nothing.

A baby may have an acute viral illness for two or three days but the problems from the cold, such as extra mucus and the congestion and narrowing of nasal passages, can last for a week or two beyond that. Then another virus can come along and get into the baby's nose or intestinal tract. Babies with intestinal viruses can get more runny stools. Breast-feeding babies can get runny or watery green stools because the bile that would normally be reabsorbed is not being reabsorbed because the stool is hurrying through. Babies who get an intestinal bug can throw up and look quite sick. During the first few weeks of life you will probably need your doctor to look at your baby if he catches an intestinal bug. In general, intestinal illnesses are easy to treat in a breast-fed baby because the treatment is nursing. Sometimes you will have to nurse more frequently for shorter intervals. You may wait for the baby to spit up or throw up. You will try to burp him more frequently.

If your baby has a cold in the first few weeks you might want to check in with your doctor but you may not need to go see him. There are a lot of viral illnesses in a baby's first year of life. And while breast-feeding babies get fewer viruses, they still get some. This can be a little disappointing for breast-feeding parents because they will call me and say, "We thought if we breast-fed, he wouldn't get sick." While they won't never get sick, they will get sick less often and their illnesses are easier to treat.

Serious illnesses are a bit easier to recognize. One of the absolute hallmarks of a serious or significant illness in a baby is a baby who refuses to breast-feed. If I get a call from parents with a three- to six-month-old who is refusing to nurse I will ask them to bring the baby in. In most cases, the baby is fine and doesn't have an ear infection, pneumonia, or other illness but it is worth checking out.

A fever in the first three to six weeks of life requires a doctor's visit. The signs and symptoms of a cold are not that different from the signs and symptoms of a severe infection at this age. When a baby this young has a fever get to your doctor as soon as possible. I do not recommend routinely taking a baby's temperature. If he feels hot to you he probably has a fever. If the baby is very young and has a fever of 105 degrees, he needs to see the doctor.

A fever, after about two months of age, can be treated symptomatically by keeping the baby cool and giving the baby long, warm tub baths. Don't worry about a fever of 101 to 103. There are no dangerous fevers or dangerous heights of a fever for a six- to twelve-month-old baby. A baby's immune system is a little bit different than an adult's and can respond in a rather uncoordinated fashion. Babies can get a fever of 105 with a cold or they can have pneumonia with a fever of 101.5. What you need to do in the case of fever is to bring the fever down—not because the fever is dangerous or bad but because it is difficult to assess a baby with a fever. A fever of 104 helps the baby fight an illness but at 104 all babies will look bad. She will be so uncomfortable she won't eat or sleep well, and it's hard to evaluate her. If the baby looks okay after you cool her down a little bit and she begins to nurse, she is probably okay. If you bring the fever down and your baby still looks terrible it is time to go to the doctor.

Parents don't need to be overly concerned about high fever in a baby. There are a lot of myths about fevers that all doctors perpetuate. We promulgate these myths by asking that question on the phone. The first question to the mother usually is, "What temperature did you get?" or, "How high is his fever?" In fact, even though in adults the height of a fever may be correlated with the severity of the illness and a 105-degree fever might be the sign of a much more serious illness, in children this is usually not the case. High fevers do not lead to seizures any more than lower fevers do. About 140 to 150 kids in the first year of life will have a seizure with a fever because there's a point in the brain that's very sensitive to temperature elevation. This doesn't appear to be correlated with the height of the fever or the severity of the illness, but it is a benign condition called a *febrile seizure*. But the reason to bring down a fever in a baby at 105 degrees is, first, because the baby is very uncomfortable, won't eat, won't sleep, and it's hard to keep the baby well hydrated. Second, it's very difficult to assess a child with a 105-degree fever because they will look terrible. When you bring the temperature down with Tylenol-like medicine, or a long, lukewarm tub bath, the fever comes down and for about one-half hour to an hour you can see your child again. You can see that obviously it was not a serious illness, it was a big fever with a small underlying illness. It is worth lowering the temperature mainly for that reason. Again, fever is not dangerous for children. However, during the first three or four months of life, fever is much more significant and those babies should either be seen by a doctor or discussed with your doctor.

If a baby is nursing poorly, not gaining weight, and having fevers, I might think he has a urinary tract infection. Breast-feeding babies do not usually get urinary tract infections but if it does occur it has to do with a variation in anatomy, such as a narrowness of the urethra or reflux of urine backward that causes the infection. These things usually require a specialist's care.

Summary

One of the hottest topics today in all pediatric offices, in lay literature, and in medical literature involves vaccinations: how many we need; when we need them; do we need more; do we need fewer. Read this chapter along with everything else you can find because the subject of vaccination is controversial and you, the parents, should know both sides of the argument and then make up your own minds. Childhood illnesses are very common. In an average winter there are about two hundred separate viruses that circulate. Your baby is new to these viruses. All babies pick up these viruses and they toss most of them off. Breast-feeding babies get fewer illnesses and get better quicker when they get the illnesses. There are virtually no illnesses that I see in my practice that really threaten the child, but many illnesses are long and I have to help the parents get through them.

CHAPTER TWELVE

Trust Your Instincts

The words I tell parents to live by are, *nobody knows your baby better than you do*. When you are pregnant you may have some concerns about whether or not you will know how to do the right things. You will be extremely pleased at how quickly instincts kick in. You know how to hold your baby, feed your baby (maybe with a little help), and respond to your baby's cues and sounds and cries. Many books and well-meaning friends and family members will tell you to do things that go against your instincts. They may tell you to feed your baby on a schedule or teach your baby to soothe himself to sleep rather than sleeping in his natural rhythm. You know to hug your baby and listen to your baby. A baby who is crying is talking to you about a need for hunger, warmth, comfort, and trust. Don't ever worry about spoiling your baby. You cannot pick your baby up too much. Your baby doesn't need to wait to eat—he needs to eat when he is hungry. It's not nice to ignore your baby yet that is what people who say "let him cry" are telling you to do. He won't be spoiled if you listen to him and respond appropriately.

Parents' instincts are good. As far as your baby's intellectual development and the growth of your baby's vocabulary and mind are concerned, your instincts will lead you to talk to your baby. Babies listen closely. They might not understand the words and they might not speak but they understand that you are respecting them as thinking people. They might not understand the words but they do hear your tone of voice and that you are interacting with them. In the brain is something called the *reticular activating system* or the *reticular activating process*. This is an overall networking by which the brain connects different parts of the brain. It is working at birth and it works throughout our lives. I ask parents to explain everything they are doing to their baby. I do it throughout a check-up. I will tell a three-hour-old baby, "I'm going to look at your eyes now." Obviously this baby does not know what I am saying, but she understands that someone is talking to her. And, while she may not be storing the exact words or information that I am talking about she is taking in the sense that someone is treating her with respect as a thinking, feeling being. Babies are understanding and taking in a lot more information than we think they are, and it is one of the nicer and more scientific reasons for talking to babies as soon as they are born (perhaps even before birth) and telling them everything we are doing, and to continue talking to them as they go through the first year or two of life. This is because they are taking in the information, processing it, and it is being stored in their brains in ways that we may not know anything about.

If you ever have any doubts about your baby you should be sure to ask your doctor. But remember that your instincts should not be ignored. During my first year of practice, some very nice people brought their four-month-old to my office. I was the third doctor they had seen and they said, "We want to discuss the baby's hearing with you." I clapped my hands very loudly and thought I saw the baby blink. I talked loudly and thought I saw the baby paying attention. Then I said, "I think everything is okay and I think we should wait another month." The mother didn't reach out and grab me by the throat (although I could see that she wanted to). All she said was, "Listen, we know our baby can't hear. We've come to you to get a referral for a hearing impairment evaluation." As it turned out this baby actually was deaf. The parents knew it and I have never felt worse than I did when I did not listen to those parents. What I learned from this experience is that I need to pay close attention to what the parents are thinking and feeling about their child. What any parent can learn from this is to trust their instincts and not let their fear sit around without taking some kind of action that will give them satisfactory information about the situation.

Most parents worry about one thing or another and in most cases I can reassure parents that their worries are unfounded. Your doctor needs to be able to listen to you, take your worries seriously, and give you information that helps your worry go away.

Some parents' fears come from not knowing what realistic expectations are. If they expect their baby to be born with a cute little round head and a smile on his face and instead they have a baby with a cone-shaped head and an impassive expression, they might be worried. If I can educate parents about realistic expectations then I can take some of their worry away. This book and other books about development written by Dr. Sears and Dr. Brazelton show that babies develop in a variety of ways. Dr. Brazelton's book *Infants and Mothers* describes how he took three different babies—a quiet baby, an active baby, and an average baby—and tracked their development. He simplified it very nicely and it's a fun book to read because it talks about the ways babies go through the first six to twelve months of life. Some babies seem to sleep all day. Other babies seem to be up and just take catnaps and only sleep in one- or two-hour bursts at a time. Some babies sleep much longer. Some babies are very, very interested in the world from the first five minutes on and just don't seem to lose interest. Other babies take weeks and weeks and weeks to tune in to your facial features. And all of these babies are normal. One of the things I ask parents when they tell me how long their baby sleeps, and often it's a baby who sleeps more than they expected, is, "What is the baby like when he is awake?" If the baby is wide awake, eager to nurse, and eager to make eye contact as best it can during the first weeks and months of life, that baby is okay. A baby who appears apathetic, isn't interested, and sleeps a lot is a different issue altogether.

I remind parents that there is a tremendous variation among babies. Most four-month-olds do not roll over well. Very few six-month-olds sit up really well. Babies do not sleep through the night in the first year of life. They do not love solid food at seven months of age. Very few one-year-olds are good at walking. Many can walk, they are just not very good at it. They do not like to wean themselves at nine months of age. I use weaning in the European sense meaning decreasing breast-feeding and increasing solid foods. It doesn't mean the cessation of breast-feeding the way we use it in America. I think that weaning is a long, slow process in which solid foods can start at six to nine months of age that continues all the way through twelve, twenty, or thirty months or however long a mother wants to breast-feed her baby. In America we have very, very unusual habits about breast-feeding, habits which are not followed in most other countries. We have a very short duration of breast-feeding and an attitude that it isn't important after six to twelve months. Nutritionally speaking, breast-feeding may decrease in its crucial aspects when the baby is eating a great diet at ten to twelve months of age, even though it's still the preferred food. Immunologically speaking, however, breast milk and breast-feeding retain all of their crucial importance during the first twenty-four months of life at least. Baby's immune system is far from mature at eighteen to twenty months of age. Baby's immune system is far from able to respond as well as ours to certain viruses and bacteria, and with breast milk these babies do much better than without it.

Not all babies get their teeth at the same time. A baby can begin teething at three to five months of age. Teething is painful. The gums swell and sometimes you can see a blister or blood blister as the tooth comes through. It disrupts the baby's days and especially disrupts the baby's nights. They will wake up more and need lots of extra hugging and nursing. A teething baby will be reluctant to breast-feed. A great thing to give a teething baby is a frozen washcloth. Get it soaking wet, freeze it, rub off the rough edges, squirt it with some breast milk to make it taste familiar and give it to the baby to chomp away on. The cold will numb the gums and the hardness will help the teeth break through. I also recommend homeopathic teething tablets because they work so well. If your baby is particularly troubled by teething you can give him some baby Tylenol.

At nine months of age I usually tell parents to listen to

their instincts even more. Many parents transfer to my practice when their child is nine months old because their doctor is not supporting their instincts on attachment parenting. I let parents know that up to nine months, many people will tell you how *they* want you to raise your baby. At the nine-month mark they will start telling you about a lot of "shoulds." Your baby *should* be sleeping through the night, your baby *should* sleep in her own bed, and your baby *should* be eating different foods from what you are feeding her. I encourage parents to trust their instincts, nod politely, and continue to do what they are doing. Of course these are the same people who will look at your wonderful, healthy nine-month-old and say, "What a great baby. You certainly must be lucky!" You know that while there may be a little bit of luck involved, your baby's health has more to do with the hours of love, care, devotion, and listening to your baby that you have put in.

My overriding philosophy in this book is listening to your baby. Babies talk very plainly. When a man and a woman have a baby, obviously their lives change dramatically, and in America and in other countries, people try to get you back to the way your life used to be as quickly as possible. First, there is a new reality and a new normal status because of the baby. The amount of rewards is commensurate with the amount of work that you put in, unlike a lot of other lines of work like being a doctor, lawyer, or agent, but it's hard work and to deny this as is done in the simplistic parenting books—

books about getting your baby to sleep longer or getting your baby to fit into your life right away—is to deny how different it is going to be and how occasionally difficult it is going to be, and does a disservice to new parents. As a result, a lot of parents fight everything that happens and they don't have much fun. Doctors can be just as guilty with the "shoulds." During medical training there are a lot of stock answers that doctors and pediatricians are taught and then we repeat them to the parents as truth. The truth is that there isn't anything dangerous about attachment parenting. You can't over-love, over-hug, or over-cuddle your baby. A baby who is sleeping in your bed doesn't learn anything except that he can get the extra warmth, trust, and cuddling he needs. Any habits can be broken. If you decide you don't want your baby in your bed anymore after nine months or a year you are going to go through a hard week. I don't know why people want to go through this separation in the first week. I advise choosing the fortieth or hundredth week for changing a baby's behavior.

Listen to your baby and listen to your instincts. Nobody will ever know your baby better than you do. If you think something is wrong, do not let anyone talk you out of doing whatever you need to do to make sure nothing is wrong. If you listen to your baby and follow your instincts you will not be disappointed. In fact, you will be rewarded greatly for the time, love, and effort you have put into raising your child.

You will have a healthy, happy baby, and it doesn't get much better than that.

Summary

I would like to repeat over and over again: You know more than you think you know. As soon as you have your baby your instincts will kick in and you'll know how to hold your baby, you'll know how to feed your baby, you'll know how to change your baby, you'll know how to respond to your baby—until somebody gets in your way and tells you not to listen to what it is your baby says. Don't listen to that person who tells you not to listen to your baby!

A–Z Conditions and Concerns

Abdominal Pain A baby can double or triple his weight in the first six to twelve months of life. Even though breast milk is the "perfect food," stomach cramps and lots of gas will make him look very unhappy. This is normal. Viral flu bugs can also make for tummy pain and may need to be discussed with your pediatrician.

ABO Incompatibility If a mother has type O blood and her baby is born with type A or B because of the dad's genetic makeup, increased jaundice can result. This is almost always a benign condition in healthy, full-term babies.

Accidents Please don't let anyone ever drink hot coffee or tea within five yards of your baby. Ten yards is a safer distance.

Adoption Many families choose adoption as the best option for having a baby. This special circumstance does not preclude the possibility of breast-feeding or bonding and attachment during early hours in the hospitals.

Alcohol Reasonable amounts of beer or wine may be consumed while you're breast-feeding. Reports to the contrary are not based on good science, and may discourage nursing moms from enjoying a glass of wine with their dinner.

Allergy Many babies are sensitive to cow's milk protein, feathers, dust, peanuts, and other things. The "cleanest" possible breast milk will help, and environmental measures will also minimize early allergies. The longer a baby is exclusively breast-fed, the fewer allergies he will develop and the less severe they will be.

Asthma As with allergies, asthma can be minimized by prolonged breast-feeding and environmental controls. Another name for asthma is "reactive airway disease." If it is dusty or smoggy enough, anyone might wheeze. People with asthma wheeze at a lower level of irritation. Medications can control asthma that can't be controlled in other ways.

Bath Time Daddy time. Dads should sit in the tub with their babies whenever possible. Be very careful: Never leave a baby unattended for even a few seconds, for any reason. Test the water and make certain that your hot water heater is set close to 120 degrees and not higher to avoid accidental burns.

Birth Defects These are rare. Birthmarks and small variations are relatively common, and many birthmarks are temporary.

Bowel Movements Breast-feeding babies never have solid stools and they are often mistaken for diarrhea by new parents. The color varies from green to brown, yellow, or orange and the consistency is "mushy." Some babies will poop with each feeding during the first days and weeks but most babies slow down a lot by the end of the sixth week, and it's not unusual for a breast-feeding baby to skip days between bowel movements. A formula-fed baby having harder stools less frequently needs attention. A breast-feeding baby having a poop once a week is normal.

Breast-feeding This is the optimal way to feed a baby and a mother's health is also measurably improved by nursing. Nurse early and often after birth and never allow a hospital staff to give your healthy, full-term baby any bottles at all. Even one bottle given by a night-shift nurse can trigger allergies in later childhood while discouraging the early initiation of breast-feeding.

Car Safety An infant or toddler not fastened into a car seat is at high risk for injury or death during even a minor car accident. Never travel without having your baby properly buckled in. Get whatever help you need to make certain that the car seat is properly installed. Most of them are not.

Check-ups I build my relationship with a family and with a baby through regular office visits. They are worth your time and trouble. Each visit with your doctor should be unhurried and all your questions should be answered. Doctors are your employees and sometimes we forget that. If that happens, slow the doc down and get all the information and answers you need before he or she walks out the exam room door. Settle for nothing less.

Circumcision If you can avoid doing a circumcision, do so. The purported medical benefits come from studies that were not done very well; however, the decision is exceptionally personal and is your own. The rate of circumcision is very low in virtually every country in the world except the United States. Even in America the rate has dropped to the point where your "intact" son will not be the only one in the locker room.

Colds Viruses cause nasal congestion, and babies are not very easy to treat. Upper respiratory infections (colds) last for days and sometimes they seem to last for weeks because babies and children can get three different germs in rapid succession. Cool, moist air is the best treatment. Antibiotics may help to shorten or even cure a bacterial illness but they have absolutely no impact on a viral infection.

Colic This is a large problem. Babies cramp and cry and nothing seems to make them feel better. We're still not sure what causes colic but it seems related to irritability of the bowel during adulthood. The word *colic* is used completely incorrectly to describe babies who are not being fed often enough or picked up often enough. These babies cry but the solution is fairly easy: Hug your baby, feed your baby. Throw away books that counsel letting your baby cry. Real colic is quite rare. I see a case or two each year. I see babies who are not getting enough attention every week. The latter problem is quite solvable.

Coughs Irritation from a cold or other infection causes mucous to drip and this has to be coughed up. Again, cool, moist air is the best treatment along with positioning a baby upright or at a slight angle when they sleep. Cough and fever should be discussed with your doctor during the first few months of life. Pneumonia is a "lower respiratory tract" infection and may need your doctor's care. Hot, dry air makes things much worse for most kids.

Cradle Cap The scalp secretes oil, and when excessive amounts dry and stay on the scalp it gets flaky and looks yellowish in color. I treat this by rubbing a little jojoba oil and a little aloe vera into the scalp and then lightly scratching it off. Cradle cap can last a long time but is quite harmless.

Crib Death Also called Sudden Infant Death Syndrome or SIDS, this is every parent's worst nightmare. Many preventative measures can be found such as parents and caregivers quitting smoking, breast-feeding, having a baby sleep on her back (not her side or stomach), and eliminating loose bedding, pillows, or blankets. My personal opinion is that breast-feeding and the family bed could eliminate most crib deaths.

Croup Certain viruses irritate the air passages and cause a cough with a very distinctive "barking" sound. This frightening-sounding cough is almost always a benign, self-limited (ends without treatment) disease. Like most other upper and middle respiratory ailments, cool, moist air is the best treatment. I think that I scare some parents when I recommend that they take their "crouping" infant into the car (dressed warmly), open all the windows, and drive for a half hour. This large volume of cold, wet air often will open the airways. Young babies with croup or older kids with persistent croup need to see their pediatrician. I also make certain to tell parents that the second night of croup is usually worse than the first. This is a highly contagious viral illness.

Crying Crying is meant to be stopped. Period. Listening to a baby cry and ignoring him is like listening to your most beloved friend or relative ask very important questions and ignoring him or her. Don't believe anyone who tells you that crying is "good for the lungs" or that "some babies just need to cry." I consider this unscientific and mean.

Diaper Rash The diaper area is warm and—no matter how often you change diapers—always wet. Mild irritation can quickly turn into a major rash and even a yeast infection. Keep a baby without a diaper for short periods throughout the day to "air him out" a little. I also recommend getting some grapefruit seed extract from the health food store and keeping a very diluted spray on the changing table. GSE fights yeast and other organisms, which create bad diaper rashes. Bentonite clay is another health food store remedy.

Diarrhea Frequent, loose stool is almost always caused by viruses. Breast-feeding babies manifest this with a lime green poop colored by bile, which would be reabsorbed in the intestines if the stool were not moving through so quickly. There is no "rehydration solution" even remotely as good as breast milk. There are still a few very uninformed doctors who will try to tell you that you should interrupt breast-feeding because of diarrhea and use a commercial fluid replacement like Pedialyte. Pedialyte might have a place in the care of a non-breast-fed infant but has no use in a breast-feeding family.

Drugs I get a dozen questions each day about medication taken while nursing. In spite of what the PDR says, there are almost no routine medications that get into breast milk in a quantity sufficient to affect a baby. *Not* breast-feeding is a medically dangerous thing to do. Declare yourself a breast-feeding mother and get a medicine compatible with what you're doing. Many doctors are quite uninformed about this crucial issue.

Ear Infections When I look at a child's ear, I am looking through the ear canal to the eardrum, which separates the outer ear from the middle ear. The bones of the middle ear are constantly lubricated by fluid and this fluid drains through the eustachian tube into the throat. Blockage of this tube can create a "stagnant puddle" in the middle ear, which then gets infected by a virus or bacteria. We used to believe that antibiotics worked to cure this problem but doctors have known for some time that the best thing to do is control pain during the first three to four days and consider medication later. Talk to your doctor.

Fever One of the ways that the immune system defends our bodies from infection is by elevating the normal temperature to 101 degrees to make white blood cells move faster and kill better. Additionally, viruses and bacteria don't live as well at these higher temperatures. Fever is not dangerous and does not cause brain damage. A high fever does not necessarily lead to larger problems and does not always reflect the severity of a child's illness. About one in every forty children may have a convulsion with a fever in the first few years of life. Discuss this with your doctor because he may encourage much more vigorous temperature control in susceptible children. Besides acetaminophen or ibuprofen-containing drugs, long, lukewarm tub baths do an excellent job of lowering fevers and making kids feel more comfortable. Comfort and assessment are the most important reasons for dropping the fever: A child at 103 degrees is very difficult to assess. When one lowers that temp and the child smiles and plays for a little while, it can become apparent that it was a big fever with a small underlying illness, rather than a dangerous illness.

Fontanelles These are also known as "soft spots" and are the areas of the skull that move around as the brain grows (and during delivery, too!). They are not as delicate as you've been told, and can be felt, "traced," and examined by parents. When a baby is lying down, the soft spot might bulge a little. If it's "tight" and bulging while your baby is sick, ask your doctor to discuss potential problems. Conversely, a comfortable upright baby may have a softer, more concave soft spot and this is rarely the sign of dehydration or anything else ominous. If you're worried, talk to your pediatrician.

Gestational Age This is the number of weeks after a baby's conception. Full term is forty weeks but a baby born after thirty-six weeks is usually considered "term." After forty weeks, a baby is considered "post-term" and at slightly higher risk for problems, which your doctor will discuss with you. In some families and in many women, pregnancies are longer than forty weeks and are perfectly healthy.

Growth and Development, Normal There can be a wide range of normal growth and development and the baby's appearance and physical milestones are far more important to me than height and weight. I look very closely at a baby gaining weight and not meeting normal developmental milestones. On the other hand, I am comfortable with "watchful waiting" for a baby who looks great, is developing normally but is gaining weight slowly.

Head Shape Elongation after delivery ("conehead") is normal and changes over the first twenty-four to seventy-two hours. It can look frightening while still being 100 percent normal, especially after a long, tough birth. Flattening may occur in a baby who spends too much time lying on his back. Talk to your doctor to correct this. If your baby's head shape concerns you, your doctor can either reassure you (99 percent of the time!) or act on your concerns with X rays and referrals.

Hearing The hearing tests administered in the hospital are a little controversial because some experts have disputed their accuracy. If *you* have doubts about your baby's hearing, talk to your pediatrician and don't quit until you are satisfied that his/her hearing is normal.

Hiccups Only a pregnant woman knows what it feels like to have someone else hiccuping in her body. This reflexive behavior continues through the first months of life and is completely normal and often unstoppable.

Hospital Policies and Routines Hospitals function best on routines. Slow them down and keep your baby in your room with you. (As usual, the advice here applies to healthy, full-term babies and not to premature newborns or babies with any problems.) Babies rarely need to be bathed shortly after birth and rarely need to be separated from their parents. Ask for "strict rooming-in" or "mother/infant nursing care" and make sure your hospital understands what you think is best for your baby.

Immunizations Talk to your doctor about vaccines and be certain to understand what your baby is receiving and when. The illnesses we vaccinate against are rare in the Western Hemisphere but still common in some other countries. I do not recommend vaccinating until you understand the benefits and the possible risks.

Infant "Acne" Newborn babies have lots of rashes and the one that lasts the longest and worries parents the most is acne. The mother's large amounts of female hormones, which affect a baby in the womb, are lost when the cord is cut and then come back full force when a baby begins getting lots of breast milk. An acnelike rash can begin in the first week and continue for the first three months of life. If the rash looks bad to you, ask your pediatrician to have a look. It's very rare for this rash to cause any lasting problems, but ask if it keeps getting worse and worse.

I treat infant acne by applying breast milk to the rash. The antibodies and potent antibacterial constituents of Mom's milk will help to kill the germs that can worsen the rash.

Jaundice Red blood cells break down and one of the by-products is a yellow chemical called bilirubin. In sick babies or premies, high levels of jaundice may be dangerous. In healthy, full-term babies, they probably are not. Breast-feeding should never be interrupted for jaundice and water only makes things worse. Nurse early and often and you will prevent and treat mild "hyperbilirubinemia."

Measles, Mumps, and Rubella These three viral illnesses are almost nonexistent in America but are the cause of serious illness and death in other countries. The vaccine is controversial because some researchers have found connections between the MMR and autism. These connections are disputed or refuted by the vast majority of doctors and experts. In my opinion, "the jury is still out."

Meningitis This is a rare but dangerous infection of the lining around the surface of the brain and spinal cord. I have a busy practice but I still have not seen a single case of meningitis in the past five years. This is in large measure owed to the HIB vaccine, which has almost eliminated the most common cause of bacterial (the bad kind) meningitis in babies. A very sick baby with either a bulging soft spot (fontanel) or a stiff neck must be seen by a doctor immediately.

Milk I ask six-year-olds if they drink elephant's milk. They laugh and tell me they're "not elephants!" I run through a short, funny list of animal questions and end with a cow's milk question. They get it. Adults don't. Dairy products should be a small part of a human's diet.

Nutrition The cornerstone of good medicine and yet ignored by many doctors. Make sure your doctor knows about good childhood nutrition and supports the healthy way you want to feed your baby and child. American infants and children grow up on too much highly processed, salty, greasy food. We now have an epidemic in adult-onset diabetes and adult-type obesity in children as a result. This is a truly cruel thing to do to a helpless child. Avoid the standard Western diet and feed your children better.

Pacifiers Pacifiers interfere with good infant nutrition. They may lead an inexperienced parent to try to figure out how to quiet a baby rather than figuring out what they really need. Usually, they just want to be fed again. (Again?! Yes, again.) A reasonable compromise might be to use a pacifier for a breast-feeding baby sitting in a car seat. In the early days, weeks, and months, take every opportunity you can to breast-feed your baby and avoid pacifiers.

Pets Don't leave babies and dogs alone. Cats do not endanger babies and dogs rarely do, but be careful. If there are animal allergies in the family, postpone getting a pet until the baby's older and you can see which allergies have been passed on to him.

PKU Test A genetic screening test is administered to your baby as he leaves the hospital. This heel stick screens for rare but treatable dangerous diseases and I think that it's worth it.

Postpartum Depression Hormones change during pregnancy and after delivery and many women experience "blues," mood changes, and even short-lived depression. Get help and counsel from a valued friend or health care professional and don't isolate yourself. PPD is different than the aforementioned conditions, and *always* should be brought to your doctor's attention. Medication may or may not be needed and most antidepressants are safe for breast-feeding. Prozac is questionable for nursing moms but even taking that medicine and breast-feeding is safer than not breast-feeding altogether.

Prematurity Babies born at thirty-six weeks gestational age or earlier are considered premature and at higher risk for respiratory problems, digestive problems, and infections. The newborn intensive care unit (NICU) may be your preemie's home away from home for a few days or longer and the staff there will answer all your questions. Don't let any questions go unanswered.

Rashes A baby's skin is so soft that just drooling and rubbing on a blanket can create a new rash. Protect the skin from rough things and treat mild rashes with fresh air, natural oils, and fresh aloe vera. (When you have a baby, get yourself an aloe plant. You'll need it for rashes, scrapes, and other things.)

"Ringworm" This is a misnomer for a yeast infection on the skin. It is so named because it can be circular, raised, and have a center that is clear and flat. It can look like a worm sitting on the surface of the skin. Grapefruit seed extract—*very* diluted—and fresh aloe will beat most of these mild infections. Call your doctor if the rash seems to be spreading rapidly or if the skin is beginning to break down.

Safety Concerns Sometimes babies begin to roll, squirm, and move before we expect them to. Never leave your baby unattended on a changing table or anything similar. *Never* leave your baby in or near water. Turn your hot water heater down to 120 degrees. Get small things off your floor and crawl around on the floor looking for sharp edges, corners, and electrical cords and sockets. Don't stop looking. As you crawl, imagine yourself to be a brilliantly smart baby with the common sense of a rock.

Seizures Also known as convulsions, this is a lot of random electrical firing in the brain leading to twitching, thrashing, or just staring or falling. If you suspect that your child's neurological responses are not normal, talk to your doctor. If he can't convince you that everything is 100 percent normal, get a referral to a neurologist. Normal babies are very jittery and often have what might look like convulsions in response to noise and a lot of other stimuli. Make sure your doctor sees the type of movement or behavior that worries you.

Separation Anxiety As babies get older, they don't like being away from their loved ones. They may cry, yell, or get very sad and quiet. This is almost always normal. I don't recommend separating much during the first months and I don't think that hours-long separations are healthy for a baby's emotional development.

Siblings Getting an older brother or sister ready for the baby depends on the sibling's age. With siblings under age three, start in the last months of the pregnancy and answer small questions. Older kids will want to know sooner and have to be reassured that they will not "lose their place" nor have the undue burden of showing the newcomer the best way to use the swings, slide, or playground. What might seem like fun to us only strikes a four-year-old as a pain in the neck.

Be wary of visitors who walk by the older sib on the way to the baby. The baby doesn't care about visitors but the big sister or brother can get hurt feelings easily.

Sleep Issues You will get less sleep and different sleep than you had before becoming a parent. Sleep with your baby, respond and feed your baby, and slowly decrease nighttime interaction after nine months of age. Earlier "sleep training" has very little scientific basis even though the authors of these books are more clever than I in selling the notion to you. Your child will not wake up at night forever and the extra love, warmth, and trust given during those middle-of-the-night sessions is invaluable.

Speech and Language Development Two-month-olds coo, four-month-olds have long "sentences," and six-month-olds begin to learn consonants and recognize their own names. These generalizations are reasonable but not invariable. One-year-olds usually speak a few words and understand many more. In the second year of life, most children add words to their vocabularies every week and speak in short phrases and even sentences as the second birthday approaches. The key to language development is not so much comparing your child's pace with another but making sure that there are more words spoken and understood each month of the second year.

Sun Protection Use sunscreen beginning at six months of age. I know the mom who makes "California Baby" and I'm pretty sure it's the best sunscreen out there for your baby. Find creams with the least amount of chemicals, the most "opaque" protection; apply lightly and often.

Tear Duct Blockage This minor "design flaw" leads to the backup of tears in the eye, thickening of the secretion, and occasionally, even mild infection. Massaging the tear duct—which is found at the middle corner of the eye next to the nose—will unblock it, and flushing the eye with breast milk every hour or two will also end this problem for a while. If there is a lot of swelling, thick discharge, or if the problem persists for longer than you like, talk to your doctor.

Teething There are twenty baby teeth, which come in during the first twenty to thirty months of life. Teething can begin weeks or months before the eruption of the first tooth—usually the middle lower two—and may begin as early as three to four months of age. The average baby has a tooth by about eight months of age but I have seen more than a few kids with teeth at three or four months and some whose first tooth could not be seen until they were fourteen months old.

Toys The best toy for a nine-month-old is a wooden spoon and something safe to hit. The simpler toys are the best. Babies begin to enjoy rattles in the first few months and these are great first toys. I'm not sure how much to worry about the chemicals found in plastic toys—while concerning, the research is very incomplete—but I do like wooden rattles for aesthetic and other reasons.

Travel Airplane air is dry, contains recirculated viruses, and can make you sick. Babies can travel early in life and I recommend putting breast milk in your infant's nose every ten to twenty minutes to make for as much sneezing as possible. Sneezing sends viruses and bacteria out of the body at about one hundred to two hundred miles per hour.

Bring lots of age-appropriate toys, food, and lots of extra clothes for the baby and yourself (in case you get peed on at the start of the flight. This has happened to me more than once.).

Twins Lots of fun, tremendous work, and worthy of an entire book.

Umbilical Cord Care The "latest" advice tells us not to put alcohol or anything else on the umbilical "stump" because these things slow the separation. Keep the cord dry and out of the diaper for a week or more and expect a few drops of blood for days as the cord separates and then falls off. If the cord smells funny or if the umbilicus looks very "wet" to you, ask your doctor to have a look. Occasionally, we need to cauterize the belly button with silver nitrate. This is not dangerous or painful.

Urine A baby may urinate right before delivery, shortly thereafter in the delivery room, or in a diaper an hour later. Urine output will slow a lot prior to Mom's milk coming in, and the urine will be dark on day two. Baby boys may even have orange, granular urine on day two or three and this is normal. If this persists, it may mean that Mom's milk is coming in slower than average and this has to be addressed by a lactation consultant. When breast milk is in fully, your baby's urine will be very pale yellow or clear and he or she may pee every twenty minutes.

Vomiting During the first weeks of life, call your doctor if your baby is throwing up. Spitting up is normal—the distinction may need to be explained face to face by your pediatrician while your baby is spitting—but vomiting is not normal. Older babies over-feed themselves or get viruses and vomit. Talk to your doctor if your baby does this a lot or if he does not look good in between the vomiting episodes. Stomach flu is a very common illness in the second and third years of life.

Weaning Breast-feed as long as you can. Six months is a great start, nine months better still, and heading toward the international average of four point two years might suit a few of you out there. Never let anyone convince you that "breast milk loses it value at twelve months" or that there's something wrong with a longer nursing time. It's the best thing for you and your baby. Wean later and slower.

Yeast Infections Yeast, viruses, and bacteria are normal inhabitants of a person's skin. In babies, the skin is so soft and the immune sys-tem so new that yeast may overgrow and cause a problem. I rec-ommend preventing this problem with frequent diaper changes, leaving the diaper off for a little while whenever you can, and keep-ing a spray bottle of diluted grapefruit seed extract on the chang-ing table. Yeast infections have become very resistant to the medications we used to use. I recommend grapefruit seed extract for the treatment of yeast and other minor infections because it works. Don't forget to dilute it. Ten drops in three to four ounces of water is a good strength.

I N D E X

Page numbers in **bold** indicate boxed
material.

INDEX

Pediatrician (*cont.*)
  breast-feeding, 42–43, 48
  breathing of newborns, 37, 43–44
  breech births and swollen genitals, 46
  car seats, 16–17, 173
  cephalohematoma, 41
  circumcision, 46–47, 174
  clothing for babies, 18–19, 49
  "cone head," 40, 179
  cornstarch, 17
  diapers, 17, 18, 176
  doulas, 19, 20
  ears of newborns, 42
  erythema toxin, 50
  eyes of newborns, 41, 59
  feet of newborns, 48, 49
  finding, tips for, **12–14**
  flexibility importance, 15
  foreskin of newborns, 47
  genitals of newborns, 45–48
  glans penis, 47
  grapefruit-seed extract, 17–18
  hair of newborns, 41
  hands of newborns, 49
  head of newborns, 40–41, 179
  hearing of newborns, 37, 42, 179
  heartbeat of newborns, 42, 44
  hernia in newborns, 45
  hips of newborns, 49
  jaw of newborns, 43
  kidneys of newborns, 42
  legs of newborns, 48–49
  lips of newborns, 43
  lungs of newborns, 37, 43–44
  maternity leave, 15, 134
  mouth of newborns, 43
  nose of newborns, 42–43, 69
  nursing blister, 43
  nutrition, 15–16
  products for babies, 17–18
  pulse checking, 49
  rashes in newborns, 17–18, 50, 176, 183
  retrognathia, 43

rib cage of newborns, 44
schedule flexibility, 15
scrotum swelling of newborns, 45
skin of newborns, 50–51, 80, 183
smoking, quitting, 14–15
"stork marks," 51
"strawberry marks" (capillary hemangiomas), 51
support for parents, 19–20
talcum powder caution, 17
telephone attitude, **13, 14**
testicles of newborns, 45–46
umbilical cord, 45, 187
undescended testicle of newborns, 45–46
urination of newborns, 45, 48, 173, 187
vaginal discharge of newborns, 45
vision of newborns, 41
well-child care, **13**
xiphoid, 44
See also Hospitals; Labor and delivery; Pregnancy
Pee. *See* Urination of babies
People, avoiding, 87
Personality of one-year-old, 123–25
Perspective for parenting, 81–82
Pertussis (whooping cough), 144
Pets and babies, 104–5, 182
Phenylketonuria (PKU), **26,** 182
Physical complexity of one-year-old, 126
Pitocin, 33
PKU (phenylketonuria), **26,** 182
Polio (IPV), 145, 149, 150
Poop of babies, 45, 48, 88, 93, 173, 176–77
Postnatal visit at hospital, 21
Postpartum depression (PPD), 182–83
Post-term babies, 31, 179
PPD (postpartum depression), 182–83
Pregnancy, 4–12
  alcohol during, 7–8, 172
  allergies and, 5–6, 59, 172
  amniocentesis, 11–12
  asthma and, 5–6, 172
  baby relationship, 12

Jay Gordon, M.D., has been a pediatrician for more than twenty years and is a certified lactation consultant. He is the first male and the first physician to take the International Board of Lactation Consultants exam. He has appeared on ABC's *The Home Show,* Fox's *Home and Family,* and PAX TV's *Great Day America.* He has many celebrity parents among his clients including Michael J. Fox, Cindy Crawford, Julia Louis-Dreyfus, and David Duchovny.